Pinky Swear

Pinky Swear

The Gift of a Lifetime

Dawn M. Chicilo

TreeHouse Ink
North Oaks, MN
USA

Pinky Swear: The Gift of a Lifetime
© 2000 by Dawn M. Chicilo
All rights reserved
First edition published October 2000
04–03–02–01–00   5–4–3–2–1

Cover photo by Brad Dixon Photography
Cover design by Dunn & Associates Design
Editing by Sid Korpi
Book design by Folio Bookworks and Mori Studio
"The Rose Beyond the Wall" by A.L. Frink

No part of this book may be reproduced in any form whatsoever, by photography or xerography or by any other means, by broadcast or transmission, by translation into any kind of language, nor by recording electronically or otherwise, without permission in writing from the publisher, except by a reviewer, who may quote brief passages in critical articles or reviews.

Publisher's Cataloging-in-Publication
(Provided by Quality Books, Inc.)

Chicilo, Dawn M.
  Pinky Swear : the gift of a lifetime / Dawn M. Chicilo – 1st ed.
  p. cm.
  LCCN: 00-91460
  ISBN: 0-9678920-0-7

  1. Lodermeier, Toni–Health. 2. Chicilo, Dawn M.
3. Cancer–Patients–United States–Biography. 4. Cancer in women–Patients–Biography. 5. Grief–Personal narratives.
I. Title.

RC279.6.L63C55 2000   362.1/96994/0092 B
                        QBI00–454

Printed in the United States of America

Featuring a

Discussion-Journal Guide

To Jamie Lee

"It (cancer) has taught me a lot about myself . . . and that I need to focus on things that are really important to me and not get caught up in the rat race. It's too bad to have to go through something like this to learn something like that. You hate to say it's a blessing, but you hate to see it as anything short of one."

Daniel Van House, Cancer Survivor

Contents

Foreword . . . . *xvii*

Acknowledgments . . . . *xix*

Introduction *1*

   One—*Toni* *3*

   Two—*Sisters* *25*

   Three—*"Can-ker"* *35*

   Four—*Key West* *41*

   Five—*The Beauty of Grief* *61*

   Six—*The Final Five* *69*

   Seven—*The Wound* *89*

   Eight—*Seasons of Grief* *109*

   Nine—*My Word* *133*

Letter to Reader *143*

Discussion-Journal Guide *145*

Order Form *151*

Foreword

That the journey toward life can begin with death is a concept few people have the privilege of experiencing. Dawn Chicilo has brilliantly put her thoughts to words as she shares the life-affirming journey she walked side by side with her beloved sister, Toni, in her masterpiece of detail as a caregiver, sister, friend and angel.

Having survived a cancer experience firsthand, it was not until I read *Pinky Swear* that I realized how hard it must have been on those who loved and took care of me. Feelings of anger, fear, denial and grief coupled with the joys of successes, both big and small, overwhelmed me as I relived my personal journey through Dawn's insightful book and came to appreciate what it must have been like on the other side of the fence. Dawn's recollections of the good times and the bad will take the reader on a journey of his or her own—one that will ultimately leave you laughing and crying for this gift that we call life.

If you or your loved ones have been touched by cancer, *Pinky Swear* is a must-read for learning to cope with loss and learning to live, laugh and love again. Dawn has summarized what it means to love unconditionally, and I promise you won't be disappointed . . . *Pinky Swear.*

> Christine Clifford
> Author, Professional Speaker,
> President/CEO of The Cancer Club®

Acknowledgments

To Sid Korpi, the magic of *Pinky Swear: The Gift of a Lifetime,* would not be possible without your phenomenal skills as an editor. When you wrote me and said, "*Pinky Swear* made me take further steps in my healing," my dream for this book was realized. Thank you.

A special thank you to the medical doctors and nursing staff at the Mayo Clinic and Methodist Hospital in Rochester, Minnesota, especially Dr. David J. Inwards, for his compassionate care and support; Sister Margeen of The Gift of Life Transplant House; The St. Cloud Hospital and Hospice; and Toni's cancer support group.

I would also like to thank the employees, supervisors, and managers of Wal-Mart Stores, Inc. who rallied to support my sister and our family.

Many people helped me write this book. For all of you who read the rough drafts and shared your thoughts and feelings, I am eternally grateful. I am especially thankful to my mom for living through it again.

To Christine Clifford, John C. Hotz and Pastor John Keller, I am deeply grateful for your guidance, support and wisdom.

The pages of this book could not have been filled without the help of Maureen McAvoy, who gingerly edited the first draft, espousing that she was an amateur at this, yet inspired me to continue when she wrote, "From my heart–this is truly awesome"; Lori Krawczyk and Eileen Buerman, my friends at work, for your support of me and my family; Sandy Swanson, who showed me what courage was; and Mary Jo Lohn, who in the thick midst of her own grief courageously took the plunge to provide me with a recent survivor's viewpoint. A special thank you to Jennifer and Lynn Bueltel, for their honest and valuable input regarding the format and rhythm, but most importantly, our treasured friendship.

To Captain Ben Taylor of Key West, Florida, for keeping the promise as advertised on the sailboat marquee–"We offer you Asylum." You mapped the Asylum's course and took me on a journey to set my sister, and me, free. You will always hold a special place in my heart.

To Judy Fischer, who shared each moment of this heartbreakingly beautiful adventure; I thank you, dear friend, for walking with me every step of the way. You swaddled me like you would an infant when I was paralyzed with fear, dragged me by my hair when I dug in my heels, and soared like a proud mother eagle beside me when I learned to fly. I have been blessed to share the dance of life with you.

To Alex, Chris and Scott, our children, thank you for your patience and for understanding when I needed quiet time to work on this book, instead of climbing the rocks on the North Shore of Lake Superior, or playing flashlight tag. Your curiosity and questions let me know you were interested and proud of me, just as I am of each of you. Nothing, not even authoring a book, comes close to being a mom. You are the greatest of all gifts.

To David J. Van House, my beloved soul mate. I couldn't have written this book without you because the story would have no ending. It would simply be another tale of a tragic loss. Instead, it is an inspiring story about the power of love. Our love and life together are a living tribute to my sister. Thank you, darling, for believing in me and helping to make one of our life dreams come true, and for your continuous loving commitment to us, to our children, and family. I love you.

To my sister, Toni, here we are even after death still exchanging gifts. I wrote this book for you, because of you. You taught me how to live. The only way to thank you for my life is to pass your gift along, to heal, inspire, and restore hope in others. That was your dream and now it's mine. Between you and me, I think we've got a pretty good chance of succeeding. Don't you? Love Ya! Sis

And for everything that came before and after, and for what is yet to come, I thank God for his designs.

Introduction

That summer I ran. I ran in sponsored events. I ran alone. I ran my first race with single knots in my tennis shoes—a sure sign of a novice. As I ran, people began passing me. Predictably, my shoes came untied, slowing me still further. I started to despair, listening to the stampede of approaching footsteps, of other runners.

Depressed, I almost quit. "What's your hurry?" I heard someone say. I slowed down, and only then did I notice the blue, cloudless sky . . . the long shadows of the early morning sun . . . the oak trees offering their cool shade. My pace became more regular. The clouds in my mind lifted, and I began to chat with the other women as they passed me. There were hundreds of them. From young to old, of all races, running together to celebrate womanhood. With my lightened load, I felt as if I were running on air. I crossed the finish line a winner, for reasons altogether different from having earned the best time.

As I stepped from the walking path around Lake Nokomis in south Minneapolis, cutting through the overgrown grass between the softball diamonds, I reflected on the underlying meaning behind the question I had heard as I ran—"What's your hurry?" Gently pulled from my thoughts by the peaceful image of a man walking his dog, I recognized the voice I'd heard was my own. But the lesson had been taught by someone else. To run freely through life is a blessing, to run from it, a tragedy. And as the understanding took hold, my grief unfolded. In the safety of my truck, I wept.

Chapter One

Toni

As I stand in the living room painting Toni's toenails with Loreal's Rubis Red polish, my mind flashes backwards, randomly flipping through the snapshots of my life, like someone about to die.

～

The house on Thomas Avenue had two bedrooms and was rented by a young couple with two small children and a newborn. It was one block from Lake Calhoun, now an upscale neighborhood in Minneapolis. Back then it was simply affordable. Mom and Dad's bedroom opened into the living room and had a pull curtain for a door. I liked that. It was easy to slip into their room at night. I would gently lay myself down at the foot of their bed after a bad dream and fall back to sleep.

Toni was an infant when the sirens sounded their warning of the approaching tornado. Mom hustled us into the pantry and lifted the tarnished brass ring on the wooden trap door. The electricity went out. She opened the floor to a darkened stairway below. We never usually got to go down there. Without hesitation, we clamored down the steps into the unfinished underbelly of our rented house. The basement had a dirt floor. A colony of spiders, centipedes, and mice lived down there. We gave it no thought. Mom was scared. I sensed that and to me, as a 4-year-old, that was enough to guarantee complete cooperation. Neither I, nor my brother Barry who was 8, protested when, a short time later, she left us alone, in complete darkness, holding the baby, while she went upstairs with the flashlight to prepare a bottle.

∽

The old A-frame swing set in the backyard provided hours of fun. Hanging upside down by our knees at opposite ends until someone fell was a favorite occupation. The plastic swings hung silently as we chased each other around the metal swing set. Around and around and around we went until, dizzily, we collapsed in the dirt. There was no grass to speak of. It didn't matter a bit. Kids and dirt go together.

A small deck extended off the back of the house. A

scar on the inside of my left thigh is a permanent reminder that I had never been told not to slide down wooden rails.

∽

Our parents had their hands full building a life on limited income and resources, with three children, each born four years apart. We helped as much as we could. While Mom slept, Barry and I, still 4 and 8, respectively, did some baking. He handed me a spatula and set me on the middle of the stovetop. Giving me the already baked, store-bought chocolate chip cookie, I placed it on the spatula and held it over the flames until the cookie's edges started to burn. I quickly dropped the flaming cookie into the wastepaper basket, which sat just below the kitchen window. I remember the pink sheer curtains and how quickly they caught fire. Mom never slept again.

∽

Mealtime was a power struggle. "You will eat that or go to bed hungry," was a common threat. Our favorite adult's rationale was, "There are children starving in Africa," to which we silently responded, "Well they can eat it then!" The threats didn't work. They rarely do. We'd gladly go to bed with an ache in our bellies to feel victorious. Ah, the lengths to which a child will go when he or she feels powerless. I remember sitting at the table long after everyone else was done, staring at the kitchen wall with my plate perched at an angle off the table's edge, hoping that Mom wouldn't notice my uneaten green beans threatening to skydive to the floor.

Ours was a family with three young children and no disposable income. We received a small gift or two for our birthdays and one or two more at Christmas. That was it. We played with the same toys all year long. So, eventually, the boredom drove us together. We played the traditional games of hide and seek and "you're it," otherwise known as tag. Sometimes the game went too far . . .

> *Our next-door neighbor was a single, older woman named Marge. She had red hair courtesy of Miss Clairol. I thought that was cool. We spent hours next door listening to Mom and Marge in conversation, while we eyed the box of chocolates on top of the refrigerator—a new diet candy proven to lose weight. (We were too young to understand the oxymoron.)*
>
> *Marge's live-in companion was a sheep dog—a child trapped inside a giant ball of fur. We couldn't have asked for a better playmate! We often entertained ourselves by pushing each other off the striped green hammock suspended from a frame in Marge's front yard. It is always amazing how*

much more fun you can have at someone else's house. The dog ran around the hammock, joining in. The risk of course was not simply falling on the ground, where the dog would lather you with wet kisses, but what you might land in!

Marge never locked her house. Back then, it wasn't even a thought that crossed your mind. So it seemed perfectly natural to include the house and the sheep dog in our game of tag.

The dog's long white coat shook like a polar bear's as she chased after us from Marge's front yard, barking all the way. We ran down the narrow sidewalk between our house and Marge's, quickly turning the corner and opening Marge's back door. The tight spring quickly slammed the wood screen door shut behind us. We ran through the kitchen with the black cat clock, whose eyes and tail moved in opposite directions, watching us. We ran through the dining/living room and out the front door through the screened front porch. We turned right and headed back to the alleyway between the houses, coming full circle.

The dog was brilliant! She had turned around at the back door and was nearly on top of us when we rounded the corner. Our surprised chorus of screams pierced the air, summoning our parents. They caught us running back through the house. Worse than our punishment was the new rule: Marge's was off limits.

~

As children, the one thing we knew we could count on was our summer family vacation.

Every year, we went to Battle Lake, near Fergus Falls, Minnesota, and rented a cabin. We showered at the lodge, and the outhouse was conveniently located a short distance from our unit. The white paint on the small, square cabins peeled off easily, exposing the gray, aged wood beneath. We held competitions to see who could peel off the biggest paint chip. Inside, we had running water. Cold water. The furniture and amenities were sparse. We had a table with four chairs (someone had to use a folding chair at dinnertime) and two bedrooms. Barry always slept on the camel hair sofa. We could have cared less about the accommodations because the only thing we came for was outside: a body of water as big as an ocean.

We swam from the moment the birds woke us until the dusk-summoned mosquitoes drove us from the water, the time between dousings so short we often pulled on damp, cold suits. At night, we played cards and board games.

One night, Toni, then age 2, sat in her baby doll pajamas playing with a deck of cards on the floor below us. We sat around the table playing crazy eights when someone happened to glance down. Facing the wall with her back to us, Toni had systematically tucked cards between the floor molding and the wood paneled wall, and had wedged one between each of her 10 tightly curled toes.

Discovered, she looked over her shoulder, smirking, and aware she had our undivided attention, she swung her arms like Daffy Duck, seeming to quip, "That's all folks!" The flash of the family Polaroid camera illuminated the image–the image that we, to this day, look at and laugh almost as hard as we did then. Priceless.

~

We also took yearly trips to Mom's hometown and stayed with Grandma and Grandpa in their double-wide trailer in Hendrum, Minnesota, where there was absolutely nothing for three kids to do. We walked uptown to the soda counter/post-office/drug/hardware store, all rolled into one, for an ice cream cone. The rest of the time we spent playing on the railroad tracks and chasing frogs. Dad and Barry slept in the chicken coop. Throughout the year, I always promised to write but never seemed to get around to it until I saw the dollar Grandma had sent Toni after getting a letter from her. But, more than incentive for Toni to correspond, it was one small sign of the very strong bond developing between the two of them.

~

Our life was balanced. It was good and bad. We fought hard. Barry, being the oldest, got away with

Pinky Swear

just about everything. I remember taking the blame for something I didn't do more than once, being called in from outside (where we pretty much lived) because some wrongdoing had been discovered.

We would stand alongside one another, like a police line-up, just inside the back door. With the youngest on one side and oldest on the other, I was like a bull's-eye in the middle. Our parents reasoned that Toni couldn't have done it. At age 2, she was too young. (Of course, the youngest matures the fastest and only feigns stupidity.) And the oldest, Barry, at that time 9, would have known better. Wouldn't he? Mom and Dad concluded that left me. There was only one time I remember their reasoning backfiring.

Someone had written on the bedroom wall with a crayon. Barry denied the allegation and identified me as the lawbreaker. By this time, I had lost faith in our family's justice system. I was asked if I did it. What did it matter? I knew it would be added to my rap sheet. "No," was all I said, resigned to the misdirected punishment I had learned to expect. This time, though, I was excused.

Startled out of the normal routine by this all-too-abrupt reprieve, I knew something was up. I walked out the back door with my ears dragging behind me, straining to hear Barry's alarmed response. "But it says 'Dawn!'" he proclaimed. He was a fly stuck on a NO PEST strip. I was too young to even know how to write my name in cursive.

~

We fought like siblings do. That's a given. But there were times when the fighting stopped and we simply loved one another. Standing on the front walk of the towering building, shielding our eyes from the sun's glare, we would search the windows on the 10th, 12th, or 14th floor of St. Mary's Hospital in Minneapolis, whichever floor Toni was on this time for one of her repeated bouts with pneumonia. We scanned the brick exterior until we saw the silhouette of the small child in feety pajamas framed by the window as she waved to us far below. Children, even siblings, were not allowed to visit in hospitals at that time. So we waved everything we couldn't say and, like participants in a parade, our hands never stopped moving.

~

Life moved on as it does, and we grew. We bought our first home in south Minneapolis, near Powderhorn Park. A great deal, Dad insisted. Mom called it a "dump" and cried. We rejoiced. Four bedrooms!

With the extra space came the increased distance. As we grew up, we grew apart. Soon, it wasn't cool to hang out with your brother or sister. I made friends and left Toni behind. She retaliated by tattling on everything I did. I could tell simply by how she called me home whether she had succeeded in getting me in trouble. There would be a lilt to her voice, as if to say "Gotcha!" "Da-hawn," she'd call, her voice dripping with sweet revenge. She was truly a brat at times. Eventually, I decided it was easier to have her tag along and make her earn her keep.

I remember the time we made her streak, naked, around the front of the house on busy Bloomington Avenue. We never gave our neighbors any thought until my parents heard about it. I sat on the kitchen counter in front of the screened window facing our backyard patio, talking to my friends, separated by the mesh-like jail cell bars. I was grounded. It didn't take long for us to learn the value of discretion.

Some family activities never lost their flavor. For instance, there was the perennial favorite: ice fishing on Lake Minnetonka. We would have to go to bed early the night before. The excitement kept us awake long past our normal bedtime. It seemed like we had just closed our eyes when Mom and Dad would whisper for us to wake up. Sleepily, we would resist the intrusion. "Are you ready to go fishing?" they'd ask. A jolt of joyous adrenaline struck and we would jump from our beds like it was time to open our Christmas gifts.

It was still and dark outside. The city was asleep at that hour, and heading out at 4 a.m. felt like an adventure. Dad had already warmed the car and loaded it with our gear. Bundled up against the winter cold, we set out, making two stops along the way— for fuel and bait.

With few exceptions, we would fall back to sleep. Dad and Mom would start the kerosene heater in the icehouse and wake us when it was warm. The rest of the day, we fished and played with the numeric counters Dad had installed to record the number of fish taken out of each hole.

The whole day was spent together in a space no bigger than 8 x 10 feet. We'd fish, snack, and eat our lunches. When someone had to go to the bathroom, the five-gallon "pee" bucket was brought in and everyone else had to step outside. If the fish weren't biting, we'd go outside and play in the snow, kick frozen perch, and walk around the other fish houses to see what they were catching, just like in the movie *Grumpy Old Men*.

Only once did the ice fishing turn into a nightmare, and my brother was a witness . . .

> *Dad found his land markers and began counting his paces to unload the fish house at the same spot he placed it every year. The pressure ridge was covered in snow. He had been carrying a highball glass when he fell through the thin ice. Thankfully, his elbow was extended and hit the ice, slowing his descent. He went under and surfaced in the same spot. Barry*

saw what happened and was running towards the open water when Dad yelled for him to stop. He watched helplessly as Dad tried to get out of the freezing cold water.

Using his elbow, Dad continued to break away the thin ice until he came to an area that would support his weight. At 6'2", weighing in excess of 240 pounds, and now soaking wet, he pulled himself from the lake and continued to roll over the snow-covered ice until he was some distance from the open water.

After Dad's plunge, the icehouse was unloaded from the trailer, the kerosene heater was lit, and Dad stripped down to his boxers while his clothes dried. He spent the rest of the day fishing.

∾

With four years between us, we never went to the same schools at the same time. I don't know if that was a blessing or not. I do know that I missed the M-80 that blew up the toilet at South High School. I think Barry was implicated and suspended. I wish I had been there to see that!

∾

Mom and Dad continued to work full-time. As most parents do, they thought that because we were more physically independent, we needed them less. The truth is, when children are learning to spread their wings, they need an anchor so they don't get lost. The key for a parent is to determine how to provide it when you're kept at arm's length. Many bone-tired parents learn that you talk when the teenager wants to—late at night.

∽

My brother began to hang out with his friends and it wasn't long before the typical trials of a teenager led to trouble. I remember Barry's withdrawal from the family and the mayhem that ensued. Mom was his primary defender. Toni was also very dependent on Mom, more so because my sister was always sick. I competed with her to get some of Mom's attention. I remember faking the same symptoms and leaving my parents no choice but to take us both to the hospital. I, of course, was discharged and Toni got the room.

It was inevitable that I would become Dad's favorite. Toni was Mom's baby and Barry was her cause. That gave me an opening and I took every opportunity I could get to help Dad in the garage or with the yard work. I would stand by the side of the car, fetching tools for him while he worked. My favorite was the old oil can, like the one Dorothy used on the Tin Man. "Can I oil something?" I'd ask every time we were in the garage. He liked that I was a tomboy. I loved the attention.

Although we spent less time playing together, our family continued to share mealtimes. The earlier power struggles over not eating our food had evolved into our shared obsession with getting as much as we could. We ate until we were stuffed, and it showed. Almost every Sunday, we went to the same restaurant for its smorgasbord, now known as a buffet. As children, we were picky eaters. Toni and I ate little more than plates full of mashed potatoes and gravy. Dad continually complained that he was paying this exorbitant price for instant potatoes. We needlessly reminded him that we also ate the desserts! One Sunday stands out above the rest . . .

Toni was 9, an awkward age she really never outgrew. She fell getting into the car as we were leaving for the buffet. Once there, she carried her tray with the heaping helping of mashed potatoes blanketed in turkey gravy to our table. She tripped over nothing. Her trayful of spuds somersaulted in the air, landing upside-down on the restaurant chair.

Toni dropped into the chair next to it, covering her face in embarrassment. Mom and I looked at one another across the table and successfully failed at suppressing our laughter.

As I began to mature, my adolescent insecurities grew to monstrous proportions. It was bad enough being overweight, but when my breasts began to bud, I became even more self-conscious. At a time when a daughter needs her mother, I felt like an island unto myself.

I withdrew into my own world of flawed classic middle-child perfectionism. I buried my head by excelling in school. The A's made me feel good. And my parents liked that I appeared to need little of their precious time, not knowing that I did everything they expected of me specifically in hopes of getting some attention of my own. But time and energy were limited commodities, and the squeaky wheels got the proverbial oil. I grew to become a self-sufficient young adult who equated dependency with weakness and never learned how to ask for help. That lesson came much later.

Typical of a middle child, I was the peacekeeper. I wanted everyone to get along and acted as the mediator when my sister started to rebel. Dad thanked me for my help once, and my career as a counselor was born.

Things stayed pretty consistent as we grew, until Dad had his first heart attack when he was 44. We had moved to Richmond, Minnesota, where my parents had bought a small summer cabin on Little Cedar Island Lake five or six years earlier. I was in college and Toni was attending Rocori High School in Cold Spring. The name of the school, Rocori, was an acronym for the three small towns it served—Rockville, Cold Spring, and Richmond. Barry drifted between jobs and apartments. Three satellites in orbit. Like a global positioning system, the call came and we responded. A near miss. Dad would recover, but time suddenly had meaning.

We regrouped as a family—a family aware that it may lose a member. It changed each and all of us for the better. Dad was awarded Social Security disability benefits. Mom got a job cleaning the Granite Company in Cold Spring. The phone calls increased, of course, to monitor Dad's recovery. The acuteness of the situation began to fade, as Dad's good health returned, but the volume of calls remained about the same. We had formerly ended our calls with a simple good-bye; now we said, "I love you," understanding how quickly and unexpectedly life can change course. And the waving or brief touching of a shoulder as we departed from one another's company was replaced with a full embrace, hug, and kiss. As with any tragedy, time wore on and we were pulled back into our lives, but the family bond remained stronger.

Graduations, full-time jobs, and marriages followed. Toni married first. At 5 p.m. at the St. Cloud courthouse, Toni, age 20, and Jeff, age 24, were wed by the justice of the peace. Toni had dated Jeff for four years. They both had attended Rocori High School, although at different times. I remember the first time she brought Jeff home to meet Mom and Dad . . .

> *Toni, age 16, was on pins and needles, for reasons other than first-time introductions. Jeff, towering above our Dad and wearing a beard, looked much older than Toni. Dad was very direct whenever he met a "boyfriend," often to the point of our embarrassment, and my sister feared the worst. I, of course, knew "the secret" she kept and she looked worriedly in my direction for telepathic support. I could see her relief as Jeff passed muster and they were free to go. I don't know how long it was before she told our parents the truth—Jeff was my age, 20, when Mom and Dad first met him.*

As Jeff recited his wedding vows, Toni started to giggle and laughed out loud from nervousness. They uncorked champagne at Lake George in St. Cloud and dined at the Pirate's Cove with the best man and maid of honor. Their wedding reception was held at Jerry's Supper Club in Richmond, Minnesota, the following day. And Toni announced my engagement to Steve, whom I had dated off and on since our senior year in high school. And as our lives moved on along similar paths, we were somehow keenly aware the clock was ticking.

I was 28 years old when the alarm went off on July 6. I can recall every detail . . .

There was no breeze. It was a warm and quiet summer day at Steve's family's cabin on Bean Lake in Wisconsin. I was 29 years old and Steve and I had been married for three years. We sat in the shade at the picnic table, eating a late lunch. A grilled hamburger on a bun with baked beans soaking through the paper plate, lay before me. I looked out at the water. There wasn't a ripple. The air was still. My inner tube hung on the dock, already dry. I had been floating alongside the dock earlier with my feet and hands dangling in the cool water, listening to the whir of Steve's reel as he cast for fish. It was so quiet, you could hear the insects. The boom box softly played Bette Midler's hit song, "Wind Beneath My Wings." A perfect day.

The sound of the gravel under the car approaching the cabin surprised me. The neighbor from down the road got out. "You have a phone call," was all she said. When she wouldn't make eye contact, I knew. And, with cement for feet, I followed behind her, speaking not a single word. Inside her house, I took the phone. "It's your Dad," I heard my hus-

band Steve's sister say. For the briefest moment, there was a ray of hope. I waited. "He's dead," she finished, and the light went out.

I remember it taking hours to drive to my parents' house. The closer Steve and I got, the more I dreaded crossing the threshold into the reality that Dad wasn't going to be there. Filled completely with dread, I was met by Toni. She began to cry when she saw me. I was numb and without any feelings as we embraced, until she said something that set free my grief. She acknowledged that I was always Dad's favorite and that he and I had had a very special bond. Because of that, she said, she was worried about me the most. Up until that moment, I realized, I had felt strangely disconnected from my own family. And now, given our family dynamics, I had lost my link to them. But Toni reached out and grabbed me, determined not to let me go.

~

Dad's sudden death at age 54 knocked me down; it was something that I couldn't control. No amount of studying or putting my mind to it would change the fact that he was gone. I struggled. I floundered. I lost my way. Losing a baby through miscarriage three months later spurred me to get the guidance I needed to survive the losses—a complete change for the person who had long ago perfected doing it all on her own.

For a few years following Dad's death, we held fast

together as a family. My mom moved in with Toni and her husband Jeff soon afterwards. Barry, who by now was also married, rose to the occasion, checking to make sure Mom was maintaining her car and calling her daily. Their bond got stronger. I kept in touch with my family through Toni. I still felt like I was missing a link until all three of us began having children. And before we knew it, we had found another way of relating to each other, without our Dad.

On one particular day, Toni and I sat in her backyard talking and laughing. It was another one of those perfect days. The weather was so spectacular it was the topic of conversation between total strangers. The grass was green and lush, seeming to beg our feet to run through it. The breeze gently lifted the tree branches, stirring the leaves. The sunshine warmed us as we sat on the patio with our feet up.

Toni's 9-year-old niece on Jeff's family's side, Miranda, sat with us and hardly spoke. I remember being her age, wanting to know what the women talked about. Just to hear tidbits of the conversation was enough to have a peephole into what life was really about. It was so exciting, especially if the grown-ups forgot you were there. Miranda was in her glory.

Toni was 29 that peaceful summer. She and Jeff had always wanted children and tried for almost seven years before that dream was realized. Their daughter Jamie Lee (named after Toni's favorite actress) was born on November 9, one year after I had my son, Alex.

At 9 months, Jamie was toddling around the backyard. Big sky-blue eyes and blond hair just like her mom; only Jamie had a halo of little yellow ringlets that bounced as her feet picked up speed, propelling her across the lawn.

Toni and I had both wanted children, and we both struggled with infertility or miscarriages. We sat as mothers that day, savoring our lives, without having to acknowledge the feeling with words. Alex and Jamie chased each other, falling down laughing. Every so often, one would yell for us. In the trees above, a cardinal whistled its song. I can still hear the sound of the claws scratching across the trunk of the sugar maple as the squirrels chased one another behind me.

~

Now, still standing in Toni's living room painting her toenails, my flashing mind freezes with this last image, as it melds the past to the present. And I remember us as we sat on her patio that unforgettable summer day. Toni had plopped her feet into my lap and I decorated her toes with the same color I used right now. The only difference is the blue beneath her nails. My sister died a half-hour ago.

Oh, God.

Chapter Two

Sisters

As a toddler, Toni was about the most adorable thing you had ever seen. And she was my shadow. For my seventh birthday, I got a walk-along doll, which I had successfully begged for. It was a very special gift. The doll looked like a brunette Shirley Temple. If you held her hand and walked at a snail's pace, the doll would walk with you. Yes, it was a far cry from the dolls of today that get sick and throw-up. But, at the time, it was the latest thing. And it wasn't often that our parents could afford the "cool" toys.

Then, one day after I'd had her for about one week, I discovered she was gone. I looked everywhere for my doll. How could she just disappear? I was old enough to know that she couldn't walk off by herself. But then where was she?

After searching the entire house, I began to suspect foul play. I went outside and with no real expectation of finding her, I went through the motions of looking underneath the wooden deck off the back of our house.

I was shocked to see the doll with her blue and white checkered dress and black patent leather shoes lying in the loose dirt. Oh, at least I had found her! I reached underneath and grabbed her leg. As I pulled her out, my relief turned to horror. As I held her up, her eyes opened and she looked back at me. I gasped. Short plugs of doll hair were all that remained on her ravaged head. Toni had been jealous.

"MOMMMMM!"

It was hard to stay mad at such an angelic looking child. Her short pixie-style blonde hair and blues eye made her look innocent. With my brown hair and matching eyes, no one could believe we were sisters. "Frick and Frack," as Mom liked to call us. Others simply borrowed the title of a popular TV show and called us "Tony Orlando and Dawn." The difference in our appearance lent itself well to the old you're-really-not-my-sister routine. It sent Toni into tears every time.

A picture from one of our annual summer vacations shows Toni and me standing side by side in front of the lake. Behind us on the dock, you can just make out Dad and Barry loading the fishing boat. It is early morning and the sun's rays are gentle. Nevertheless, we both squint at the camera. Unselfconsciously, our 2- and 6-year-old respective bellies protrude in our matching new-for-summer-vacation, gingham-checked, two-piece swimsuits with ruffles on top. Mine was orange and white and Toni's green and white. Mom insisted on a picture of her girls before we swam. We beamed at the camera. Life was good.

Other times, in the dark of night Toni would whisper to me that she was afraid to go to sleep. "Think of something pretty like flowers," I'd say. If she still couldn't fall asleep, I would tell her a story. And when that didn't work, I would sing to her "Hush, little baby, don't say a word. . . ."

So sometimes we were playmates, sometimes she was my baby, and sometimes she was my tormentor.

The house on Thomas Avenue, where we lived when Toni was born, had slate siding. Between the closely spaced houses, it was cool and shaded. Spiders hung out in hoards. The narrow cement sidewalk between our house and Marge's left little room to navigate. Although I wasn't claustrophobic, I did fear being trapped in "spider alley" with my sister.

Toni would wait like a hunter in a deer stand. Her ammunition was a daddy longlegs. She would pull off all but one leg and chase after me until she was close enough to launch the grenade. With my hair flailing behind me, I would race as fast as I could toward the house and safety. I get chills down my back remembering the physical sensation of when she hit her mark. And I would hysterically try to shake the spider amputee from my snarled hair, feeling the soft round body, as my hands would pass over it. It's no wonder I suffer from arachnophobia to this day.

I was older by four years so, of course, I was smarter. As we grew, I assumed the role of teacher. I introduced her to life. I remember the first time I took her to a beauty salon. It was in the '70s, so she would have been about 11 years old. She had long straight hair with a center part that had never been professionally styled. Her outgrown bangs I had cut were tucked attractively behind her ears.

We took the bus to downtown Minneapolis, another big first for her, and walked down Nicollet Mall. She was scared. I was excited. Once we were there, I waited until she was called and then told her I would be back. The look in her eyes said, "don't leave me here." I laughed. I loved it. I felt so worldly.

I knew she would look different when I returned. But I had no idea just how different. Her hair was now shoulder length. It looked blonder, fuller. It was feathered and curled. I was dumbstruck. My shock was registered clearly on my face as I surveyed her transformation. I still remember the twinge of jealousy. She looked like Farrah Fawcett. My little sister was beautiful. And she knew it.

Toni's face was beaming. She could hardly contain herself. I paid for the service with money I had earned at my first real job, as a dietary aide in a nursing home, and we walked back out to the Nicollet Mall, a pedestrians-and-buses only avenue. Only this time, Toni walked straighter and was looking at other people to see if they were looking at her. Bingo. She was rewarded. She side-glanced into every window she passed, trying to catch her reflection without being too obvious. It was her birthday, and I had given her a very special gift—a pattern that continued for special occasions or for no reason at all.

During the high school years, we drifted. Toni struggled with her attendance and grades. I had excelled at both. Having left the nest at age 17, when I returned home, I finally got the attention I craved much earlier in my life. Toni wasn't accustomed to this change in the family dynamics, and as much as she loved me, she ashamedly admitted later that she hated me then. She would sulk and pick fights. Moody and irritable, it would take her a few hours to come around. This pattern repeated itself until she no longer felt overshadowed and had become comfortable in her own skin.

We lived in different cities, after we both married, I in Minneapolis and Toni in Cold Spring, Minnesota, an hour-and-a-half drive. It was fun to plan our get-togethers. We loved holidays, and Christmas time was our favorite. Every year, we would draw names for the gift giving. Without exception, we would draw each other's name.

For the first time in my life, I had disposable income after graduating from college and starting my career as a vocational rehabilitation counselor. Steve was also doing well as a project manager for a residential construction company. While our combined income wasn't a lot, compared to the scarcity of my youth, I felt rich and wanted to share my new wealth with my baby sister.

As I shopped the racks of clothing for her present, I enlisted the sales clerk to bring my selections to the counter while I shopped for matching accessories—hat, necklace, earrings, socks, purse, etc. As the purchases were rung up, the sales clerk asked whom the gifts were for. I told her. "I wish I was your sister," she responded.

Another year, for Toni's birthday, I treated her to her first full-body, one-hour massage, followed by a foil and haircut. A new outfit later, we were ready to dine at one of the most notable steakhouses in the Twin Cities. Eating steaks with sautéed mushrooms and brick-sized baked potatoes, we celebrated her birth.

"You're spoiled," her husband Jeff would rib her. She readily agreed, loving every minute of it. We both did.

Of course, Toni and I didn't always get along so easily. I remember once when I got to her house, the tension was thick. Toni was in a pissy mood and Jeff was steering clear, minding his own business in front of the TV. She made a cutting remark to Jeff, and I looked at him with my eyebrows raised. With an almost imperceptible shake of his head, he let me know he wasn't touching it. She was in a bad mood. Sometimes I would avoid her, but this time, I took the bait. "Why are you being such a bitch?" I challenged her, "Are you on the rag or what?" Jeff nearly choked. There was a heavy moment of silence before Toni began to laugh. The direct approach. I've always liked it.

It took us some time to figure out that we didn't need to have a reason to get together. Soon after that realization, we planned a trip for two . . .

> "Get 'em off!!!" Toni bellowed at me, her face contorted with a mixture of fear and anger. She knew I wasn't about to touch the leeches between her toes, and in a split second I was out of my lawn chair (which we had smartly set in shallow water) and on top of the hill, which led down to the beach. Just far enough away so that she couldn't throw anything at me. I watched her struggle to get out of the lounge chair, wearing a hot pink swimsuit. She was five months pregnant. Even struggling, she moved faster than I had seen her move in years.

Pinky Swear

> *I roared with laughter. She glared at me as she sat in the sand desperately yanking the little bloodsuckers from her swollen toes. The sight made me cross my legs, laughing harder. As soon as I saw her begin to rise, I bolted—straight to the cabin, slamming the door behind me and trying to lock it as fast as I could. My heart was racing, my hands shaking.*
>
> *I got it locked! My chest heaved as I tried to catch my breath, the adrenaline still pumping. I waited for her to come to the door. But she was circling the cabin. I walked into the bedroom where the windows stood wide open, when all at once, she screamed. I jumped, even though I knew she was outside. All I could see was her head through the screen. We laughed like the children we used to be.*

This was our first vacation together, alone. With no distractions, we reconnected as sisters, leaving behind our lives to give time to each other. And we had a blast because no one can know you quite like a sister. It took us 29 years to get to this place. Our lives started to mirror one another's. Instead of competing, we began supporting, and we came to understand and cherish our special bond.

The memory of the look on her face when she spotted the leeches is concrete. I had no way of knowing that I would see that same expression one year later. And that it would mark the beginning of the end of our lives together. Only this time she displayed no anger. It was raw fear. And I didn't run from the hospital as she half-screamed, half-sobbed, "Get it out of me," frantically clawing at her chest.

"The tumor is aggressive," the doctor said, "we have to begin chemo immediately."

Chapter Three

"Can-ker"

It was August, about one year after our vacation. I had been having chest pains all day. Every time I took a breath, something would catch and the pain would stop the inhalation. I hadn't heard from Toni for a while, so I thought I would give her a call. She had been sick with bronchitis over the weekend and didn't sound much like herself. When I had spoken to her last, she had said she felt like shit.

"Hi Mom," I said.

"Oh, hi. I thought you might be Toni and Jeff," she replied breathlessly and my antenna shot straight up.

"Where are they?" I asked, my heart pounding.

"Oh, I've been so worried . . . " she stammered.

"What?!" I said in a controlled panic, my mind working much more quickly than she could possibly know.

"Toni's lung collapsed and I've been waiting all day to hear what's going on."

My chest had hurt as I lay down the night before. I had awakened with the same pain. This type of physical connection is something my sister and I often experienced. I remember the last pap smear Toni ever had. She had had it done the same day and time as I did, though neither of us had mentioned to the other that we were due for our annual oil change. The only difference was the 90 miles between us.

Lifting the receiver to answer or call, I was no longer stunned to find my sister on the other end. We mentally connected before we ever dialed the phone. Emotionally, our letters that crossed in the mail were duplicates of each other's feelings. Perhaps it was because we were so alike. Perhaps it was something more.

∼

Driving from my home in Shoreview to St. Cloud, Minnesota, I walked into Toni's hospital room one hour after I'd gotten the news from Mom. I could see the relief on my sister's face when I walked through the door. Her expression quickly laced with concern. They had diagnosed pneumonia—the disease that had now supposedly caused her lung to collapse. When she saw me, she thought something else was wrong and they hadn't told her. I remember her saying, "God, I thought maybe I was dying or something when you showed up." Her instincts were right.

Toni was hospitalized over the weekend, liters of fluid tapped from her chest cavity. The following Monday, I stopped at the nursing home in Cold

Spring to see our 84-year-old grandmother before going to the hospital to see Toni. Physically, Grandma was suffering from diabetes, arthritis, and congestive heart failure, but her mind was sharp.

"Grandma, you have to hold on. Toni's afraid she won't see you again," I said.

Regretfully, Grandma Ann, who had remained so close to Toni, replied, "I don't think I can." Leaning over, I hugged her.

"Well, then I'll tell Toni you love her," I replied, as I expressed my own love and said good-bye.

One hour later, I related the story to my sister. Toni was aghast. "I can't believe you said that to her!" she said, stretching the word *believe* out like a taffy pull. "She's gonna think she's dying!" she barked. Toni was pissed. I minimized it. "It wasn't as bad as it sounds," I insisted, despite knowing Toni was right.

Just after midnight, I woke with the ring of the phone. Grandma was dead.

Mom asked me to help her break the news to Toni. We walked through the hospital room door the following morning. Toni was hysterical. Crying and yelling at us, "How come you didn't tell me?" She had called the nursing home that morning to find out where Mom was. Toni's anxiety over what was taking Mom so long to get to the hospital had little to do with the clock. It was because Toni had dreamed about Grandma the night before.

Within days, Grandma was buried in the small

town of Hendrum, in the Red River Valley, where she had lived most of her life. Mom made the arrangements for her mother's funeral by phone. With heavy hearts, our family was there in spirit only because the same day Grandma died, we were told that it wasn't pneumonia that collapsed Toni's lung. It was a tumor.

The fight to save my 28-year-old sister's life began on the day Grandma's life ended. The doctors began the process of determining what type of tumor she had. I remember our conversations. Talking positive. Trying not to speak or voice the fears we felt. Denying that this could be happening to us.

Cancer. You hear about it all the time. It's become a dinner conversation topic and is quickly gaining the lead for the most common cause of death. Still, I never thought it would hit home. You never do. Until it does. Maybe it's better that way.

After Toni was diagnosed with non-Hodgkins lymphoma, and our worst fears were confirmed, I stood in the doorway of my sister's hospital room. Our eyes met and locked. On the phone, we could hide behind the words, the distance. At her bedside, we embraced. Once again locked together, two little girls, terrified of the noises coming from the basement.

"I'm scared," she whispered into my ear with a room full of people around us.

I whispered back, "I know. I'm scared, too."

We clung to one another until Jeff's discomfort with the expression of our feelings tore us apart. "It's going to be one hell of a roller coaster ride," I quickly murmured to her, promising Toni that she would not be on the ride alone. I did not know how literal the words would prove to be. But I did know that our lives had just changed forever. A moment of complete clarity.

When I arrived home that evening, Steve looked at my reddened, tear-stained face. I remember how he held his hands up to stop the flow of my words. I recognized the hand signals. They were the same ones he used when my dad died. I knew instantly that he would fail to support me through this crisis, too. He accused me of expecting the worst, leaving me nowhere to go with my fear and pain. Instead, I held my not-quite-2-year-old son. I began preparing him for what lay ahead. I explained that his favorite Auntie Toni was sick and in the hospital. Toni has cancer. "Can you say that word?" I asked.

"Can-ker," he replied.

Chapter Four

Key West

Toni looked at Jeff, eyebrows raised, questioning him for a response. His eyes quickly returned to the television. "We'll see," he said.

My blood boiled. "I'm going!" Toni declared, ending the discussion and returning my blood pressure to normal. We looked at each other and exchanged a tweak of a smile.

Northwest Flight 570 to Key West, Florida. Departing in February. Toni and I would be taking another trip for two. To the warm, sunny, southernmost point of the continental United States—a carrot at the end of the stick. A trip to plan. A goal at the end of the chemotherapy rainbow.

Key West. A city where anything goes. Like New Orleans, only instead of the muddy waters of the mighty Mississippi, you have the breaking waves of the Atlantic and Gulf knocking on your door. Where baldness on a woman is not even noteworthy.

I had been there twice and knew I would return, drawn to this vista like a homing pigeon. I told Toni of the "Asylum," a sailboat I had chartered once before. It gave us hope. It gave us a target to shoot for—February 8, just five months away.

At the same time my sister was fighting for her life, I hand-delivered a divorce petition to my husband, Steve.

Some people thought I had lost my mind when they heard the unexpected news of my decision to end our marriage. I had shared our struggles with very few people. I will never forget the phone call I received from Deb, Steve's sister.

I had been very close to Steve's family, loving them as I did my own. Deb just couldn't believe it and called to ask me why. I told her it wasn't my place to give her the details. She asked me if her brother was a monster. "We all have our demons," was all I said.

Her emotions rushing from denial to anger, Deb, a registered oncology nurse, asked me how I could do this now, with my sister needing all of her strength to fight the cancer within. The hair on the back of my neck stood up and I let the silence that followed speak for itself. Deb calmed down, though when she spoke again, her voice shook with emotion.

"I just can't believe it. I mean it's so unbelievable, I've wondered if you have lost your mind because of what's going on with your sister, or if aliens have invaded your body," she said.

Deb wasn't the only one shell-shocked by what seemed like my abrupt decision to get divorced. No one, of course, knew what had finally brought this marriage to its end. No one, but me.

It was just a few weeks after Toni was diagnosed with cancer. I tossed and turned most of the night, my worried mind working overtime. It seemed the only way I could get a reprieve from the nightmares that had begun to taunt me was to exercise. Months before, I had begun to run consistently. I slimmed down and was close to my ideal weight, at least according to the medical charts for large-boned women, which I however am not.

As I stood bent over the vanity sink brushing my teeth one particular morning, I looked myself in the eye and, as I had routinely done for months, if not years, mentally asked myself, "How much longer am I going to stay in this relationship?" Still unable to find the answer, I spat some toothpaste in the sink, thinking of the early morning run I was destined for.

At that moment, Steve walked through our bedroom, fully dressed, and moving like he was about to leave the house, while Alex, almost 2, lay sleeping in his crib. It wasn't even 6:30 a.m.

"Where are you going?" I questioned him in alarm, around a mouthful of toothpaste.

"I've got a tee time at 7 o'clock," he replied curtly. I spit.

"You can't golf."

"Why not!"

"I *have* to run," I declared, leaving no room for negotiation.

With a snort, Steve stomped out of the room, all 5'5" of him, and stormed down the stairs of our grand foyer. He was muttering to himself. When he reached the lower level, he shouted up to me, his words bouncing off the granite floor and sterile white walls— "You are the most selfish bitch I know."

I was startled out of my stupor and looked back into the mirror, catching my own eye. The extent of his narcissism loomed large before me, in black in white. Just the night before, Steve had returned home late after golfing 18 holes. With this morning's petulance, it felt as if the key in the lock turned, the shackles fell to the floor, and I was released.

It started slow, my laughter. The steam escaping the pressure cooker. Before long, I was laughing so hard it pulled Steve back upstairs, my response so different from the verbal fights that had become the norm. He stood in our bedroom doorway with his hands on his hips, puffing out his chest, ready for combat. His eyes bored into mine. I looked at Steve, his seething anger, and like a kid in church, I put on a straight face and pressed my lips tightly together to suppress my laughter for a millisecond before the corners of my mouth began to twitch upward and my smile broke. His eyes flared and I was consumed by uncontrollable giggles.

"You bitch!" the bald-headed ankle-biter hissed. I

pressed my lips together for a second time, trying to hold back the monsoon of laughter that was coming. The sight befuddled and infuriated him. Unable to comprehend this sudden change in our relating, he spun on his heel and stormed out of the room, again. In that brief sliver of time, the decision had been made. I was ready to leave.

Days later, Toni was released from the hospital, weak from her first chemotherapy treatments. She sat in the wheelchair as I pushed her down the empty, quiet streets in the small town of Richmond. I wanted to ask her something and needed to get her out of the house and away from Mom's watchful eyes.

"I'm going to divorce Steve," I announced. She wasn't surprised. I asked her if she wanted me to wait. After all, I had lived for seven years in this unfulfilling marriage, what would another year matter? Toni was firm in her reply, "No. I want you to be happy now."

My divorce ran parallel to Toni's cancer therapy. But instead of amplifying my emotions, it calmed them. What really mattered was clearly in focus. And as hellacious as the divorce was, it paled in comparison to her journey. Part of me wants to relive her journey because, looking back, it seems surreal. You have no doubt heard that cancer is ugly. Chemo is even more disturbing.

Chemotherapy. Let us treat the body with a highball of drugs that does not select what it will damage on the road to fighting the cancer. As you listen to someone you love throwing up nothing and crying because they are so sick, you want to scream. When you see the top layer of her tongue missing because of this "treatment for cancer" you want to rip the collective heads off of the medical profession, to scream, "Don't tell me this is helping her. Listen, it's killing her." But somehow you get used to that section of the roller coaster ride and your stomach ceases to flip over when the track plummets without warning.

～

How do you do it? Humor saved our sanity. It also made the ride more bearable.

"Ciao!" Toni quipped, waving her hand in a goodbye gesture from her hospital bed. Our lower jaws came unhinged. Jeff and I looked at each other in shock. "I always wanted to do that," she said, as Dr. *Chow* left the room. The tugging smiles turned to smirks, as Dr. *Chow* would come and go. As the door swung closed behind him, our mirthful laughter echoed in return. Poor guy.

The power of laughter. Studies document the positive effects it has on our immune system. Laughter increases circulation, bathing tissues in oxygen and nutrients. Good hormones are produced and infection-fighting cells are deployed. Recognizing this power, hospitals and cancer facilities are adding humor programs. The corporate world is hiring humor consultants to help employees deal with stress. In Bombay, India, there are laughing clubs.

But the power of laughter does not diminish the importance of tears. Crying lowers blood pressure and relieves emotional and muscular tension. By crying, we can let go of what is weighing us down.

Like siblings, joy and sorrow are related. So we laughed until we cried. And vice versa.

∽

Shortly after Toni's first batch of chemo, she sat at home waiting to lose her hair, while her body recovered from the nuclear bomb they had set off inside her. The doctors told her that her hair would fall out in two to three weeks. I swear she hung onto it out of sheer determination not to be bald for Jamie's baptism. As anyone with experience will tell you, it is physically painful when you start to lose your hair. The nerve endings seem to be on fire and the slightest breeze or movement causes pain. Maybe that's why the gal in the turban shop told Toni that losing her hair wouldn't be as hard as she imagined. She was right.

The evening after the baptism, I sat on the patio with Toni and Mom. Toni's hands repeatedly reached into her short blond mane of hair, pulling out handfuls. The reality hit us. I didn't want her to feel this alone, so I reached over and grabbed some, too. How odd it was to pull it out of her head. The strangest sensation. Soon we all started to pull. She had had it. We got as much as we could, stuffing it into a zip-lock bag (my suggestion), to match it to a wig. She looked sick then. I was scared. But by the time I woke the following morning, Jeff had plugged in the shaver and buzzed the rest off. Her makeup was on and she looked just like my baby sister. Hairless, of course.

The doctors described Toni's particular type of non-Hodgkin's lymphoma as "aggressive," so it seemed natural to move her treatment from a city hospital to the Mayo Clinic and Methodist Hospital in Rochester. Just knowing that she would receive in- and outpatient treatment from the same doctors that treated presidents and kings reassured us that the care she received *was* the best in the world.

By November, three months after her diagnosis, I was separated. We were in the process of divorce and were negotiating how to divide our assets, which included three businesses—two construction-related companies and a vocational rehabilitation consulting firm. Being self-employed, I transferred the majority

Key West

of my case files to another counselor in our office and spent most of my time handling administrative tasks. Our parent calendar afforded me scheduled time off, when Alex was with his dad, to commute from the Twin Cities to Rochester, to be with my sister. The hour or so drive to see Toni was always filled with anticipation. The trip home was filled with the songs from Vanessa Williams' CD entitled, "These Are The Sweetest Days." Inevitably, my tears began to roll when it came to the last song, "Long Way Home."

~

During one of Toni's inpatient stays, we learned that even the best medical treatment couldn't prevent the highballs of drugs from causing temporary deafness. We had to scream to include her in conversation. Needless to say, we quit conversing. It was a very quiet, depressing day in the hospital. Until Amy showed up.

Amy is my mom's best friend. A laugh a minute when she's trying. Even when she's not.

Mom and Amy decided they'd head downstairs, which was the covert language for "I need a smoke." Amy jumped up from her chair and followed Mom out of the room. Within seconds, the emergency staff descended upon us. They raced into the room with life resuscitating equipment. They found Toni, Jeff, and me staring at them in alarm. As we tried to figure out what happened, more staff piled in behind. All the while, Toni was screaming, "What's going on?" She couldn't hear a damn thing. Apparently, when Amy jumped up from her chair, it slid backwards, rocking against the emergency call button.

"What?!?" Amy wanted to know after they returned. Just seeing her made us convulse with laughter.

The treatment schedule was mapped out and revised as white blood counts, platelets, and all the other bodily ingredients being measured, dictated. Throughout this time, we supported one another and continued to find something to laugh about.

We sat in the hospital room one day when Sally Struthers was appealing to viewers to donate money for the starving children. Toni was lying in bed, starving for life. Jeff looked at a hefty Ms. Struthers turned and said, "I think she's eating those kids." More laughter.

Around this time, however, Steve told my closest friend and coworker, Judy, that he was either going to kill himself, or me, and I was granted an Order for Protection and a fragment of reassurance that I wouldn't lose my life leaving this marriage. He would later insist that he never said that, forgetting that I had called him in a state of panic, after I learned of his threat, asking fearfully, "Steve, are you going to kill me?" The only thing I heard was a long, heart-piercing silence, followed by a short click, as he hung up on me.

What followed was anything but funny. The point of sharing it at all is to illustrate my sister's capacity to care. While she's battling for her life, I'm receiving cards and letters of support from her. Not weekly, but almost daily.

One card read, *"The other day I took a long, hard look at my life . . . Perhaps you heard the scream that followed."*

Another said, *"What I want to know is this: How can I be expected to put discipline and order in my life . . . when I can't even control my hair?"*

And my favorite, *"Just wanted to let you know I'm still alive . . . Ha Ha Ha Ha . . . Have a nice day . . . ."*

In addition to these words, she wrote words of encouragement, support, and love. And she addressed every single card, *"Dear Sis,"* and signed each—*"Love Ya! Toni."* I know because I saved them all.

By no means was I the only recipient of her love. She sat waiting for a chemo treatment with an elderly woman who admired Toni's wig, the naturalness of the synthetic hair. Toni took off the wig and gave it to her. Wow.

~

During intermission between Toni's chemotherapy treatments, life continued. I vividly remember one particular day . . .

> *Jeff and I were racing around St. Cloud like contestants on "Beat The Clock." Toni, weak, tired,*

and nauseous from her most recent chemo, sat quietly with her eyes closed and head against the passenger-seat headrest. We were shopping for a radar detector so I could drive faster. As we darted across Division Street, from the Crossroads Mall to Best Buy, we almost caused an accident. Toni lifted her head, opened her eyes, and looked first at Jeff, and then at me. "What's your hurry?" she said pointedly.

―――

Toni's cancer therapy continued. It would follow a prescribed course and then be changed with no more than a moment's notice because of her response, or lack thereof, to the treatment. Our family couldn't make any plans for the future. We had no choice but to live day to day.

The roller coaster is hard to ride. You have to know when to hang on and when to let go. And sometimes you get thrown from the car. If you can talk from your heart and share the frightening moments, it enriches your life like nothing else can. What once mattered, no longer does. You are facing life and death. Your perspective is razor sharp. But you need other vents to let the steam escape because the pressure builds.

I ran. I ran as often as I could. The exercise released the physical tension. I kept a journal, writing about my fears, my feelings, and my life. This made them solid. It also helped me to see patterns.

Moments of hopelessness, followed by days of undying faith. Those words helped me then, as they help me now. It's a practice everyone could benefit from. As is seeing a good therapist. And, of course, my sense of humor carried me through. But it could never replace the support I received from someone I trusted. Someone I loved. Without that, I wouldn't have made it. Thank you, Judy.

Judy is my best friend. I tease her she could be my mom and she retorts that we are of the same generation. "We're only 10 years apart," she cleverly points out.

After college graduation, with a master's degree in counseling, I began working as a vocational rehabilitation counselor with a private rehabilitation firm in St. Paul. The company was growing and our receptionist, Eileen, a long-time friend and coworker, was leaving to stay home and raise her children. We placed an ad for an office manager. Judy responded and, after checking her references, one of which was Carlson Company, I recommended to the owner of the firm that we couldn't afford not to hire this woman. Judy's references were on fire she was so hot.

I remember when she first started. Her work product was nearly perfect. Her phone repertoire increased referrals. The clients and staff fell in love with her. She was friendly, humorous, energetic and genuinely interested in everyone's story. Judy had a heart of gold. She still does. And everyday at lunch, she left the office and sat in her car crying over her separation from her 6-month-old son, whom she had had to put in daycare. When she shared this with me, I was intrigued. Sharing her feelings seemed to come so easy to Judy. And it didn't take long for that to become a two-way street.

We worked together for nearly three years before I decided to start my own company—Chicilo & Associates, Inc.—a private vocational rehabilitation consulting firm. I remember what would have been considered my last day of contractual work with my former employer. I wasn't in the office, as my intention to start a competing business had resulted in legal action against me. Instead, I was sitting at the picnic table at Steve's family's cabin in Wisconsin, with a grilled hamburger on a bun with baked beans soaking through the paper plate when the neighbor came to tell me I had a phone call. It was the same day my dad died.

I dedicated the success of my business to my dad and poured myself into it. It was a place to hide from the grief and pain. When I'd become pregnant and, three months after my dad's death, learned there was no fetal heartbeat, I sought professional help, with Judy's assistance and unfailing support. My therapist guided me through the grief process, starting first with the loss of my dad, then my baby. Judy continued to work with my former employer, despising the owner more each day for the additional grief he was bringing me in the midst of the death of my father and unborn child. I ultimately settled the lawsuit and, within one year, Judy and I were back together. I remember the phone call that precipitated this reunion . . .

> *The phone rang in my four-season front-porch office, where I sat working at my desk: I answered it, "Chicilo & Associates," acting as both a receptionist and counselor. Judy was crying on the other end.*
>
> *Between gulps, Judy was able to tell me she had just quit on the spot and walked out because of one more asinine thing the owner had said or done. I was elated.*
>
> *"That's great!" I exclaimed. My response was so unexpected, she stopped crying, completely confused by it. "Now you can work for me," I said. And we have worked together ever since.*

From my front porch (where we worked by phone and modem), to an office in Roseville (where Steve and I, still married at the time, had adjoining offices), to a Class A building in North Oaks (an affluent St. Paul suburb where we still reside), Judy and I have stayed together.

I wouldn't trade Judy for a winning lottery ticket. Many people have told me what I already know—"She's worth a million bucks." I remember when one of our vendors asked if Judy could work on a temporary basis for them until they could find a replacement as they were really in a bind. After they found someone to fill the vacancy and Judy was no longer temping, they called me and said, "It feels like the sunshine left our office." I couldn't describe her better.

For many years, Judy was the only person that made me feel not so alone. She taught me about trust and unconditional love. Judy's life had followed a similar path to mine, and she gently guided me through the emotional mine fields. I remember saying to her, "If it's [my marriage] like this a year from now, I'm getting divorced." With a straight face, she said nothing. But the look in her eyes said it all. I groaned, "I said that last year didn't I?" With a tender smile, she had nodded her head slowly.

Outside of all the heavy stuff, and there's been plenty, Judy and I have had a hell of good time laughing at ourselves, other people, and life itself. I remember sitting in my office talking with Judy, who sat across my desk from me. As I was talking, she started to sink from view, her mouth hanging open, as the legs on her chair bent underneath the seat and she, still seated, slowly collapsed to the floor. It took me years to get around to fixing that chair because every time we looked at it we had to laugh. And we have done our share of laughing.

An insurance agency rents space next to ours. The owner, a wild haired, all-work-and-no-play business woman, walked into our office once to ask if we were having a party, or what, because she couldn't hear herself think with all the laughing that was coming from our suite. Judy, who only moments before had returned to her desk after guffawing with me in my office, looked at her innocently, with brows knit, and said, "It's just the owner and me here." The woman left, rebuffed and perplexed, questioning whether the sound could have come from the heating ducts. As soon as she departed, Judy reappeared in my office, where I had stood listening to the comic exchange. We took one long look at each other and clamped our hands over our mouths to muffle our laughter. When one of us snorted, we both made a bee-line for the door, knowing full well we'd never be able stifle ourselves, as we raced to the far office in our suite, tears of laughter streaming behind us.

When Toni was diagnosed with cancer, Judy wrapped me in her arms and held me tightly. She didn't release me until I let go of some of the heart-wrenching pain I was feeling and she could share my burden. With eight sisters of her own, it wasn't hard for her to empathize.

So historically, Judy and I go way back. And without her, I don't honestly know if I would have survived my sister's journey. I do know that February 8, the date Toni and I were suppose to fly to Key West, a carrot at the end of the stick, a goal at the end of the chemotherapy rainbow, was slipping further away into the irretrievable past.

～

After each chemo treatment, our hope was for the tumor to break up and for remission to follow. It did not. Each time, the cancer grew back faster than before. Soon, we were facing her only hope of survival—a bone marrow transplant (BMT). The doctors recommended massive chemo to buy enough time to perform the BMT. She was getting platelets on her 30th birthday, a transfusion on Valentine's Day, six days past our now cancelled trip to Key West. Not what one normally expects on those occasions.

The preparation for a BMT is unbelievable. Bone marrow sampling—a trip to hell and back. Toni recognized the nurse performing this inhuman procedure. She began to refuse to go through with it, but Jeff insisted that it wasn't the same nurse that performed the first bone marrow sampling, months earlier. Observing this exchange, after the procedure was complete, the nurse asked her about it.

Toni told her that the nurse who did the first sampling was "a real bitch." Smiling, the nurse couldn't help but respond, "That was me."

～

Amazingly, we adjusted to the nightmare and began

to treasure this new life even with death looming near. We forgot what it was we used to worry about. All of the plans we made were tentative. But we made them anyway. And we continued to laugh. Dark humor was the funniest because things were bleak. But it was humor nonetheless.

With the level of emotional stress I had, my id took over and I remember trying to plan a trip with a man I was seeing, primarily for the physical release. Judy and I laughed our asses off when I said, "With my luck, Toni will die right before we are supposed to leave and I will never get laid."

And so the dance of life returned. But with Toni's unpredictable future, the songs changed quickly, or stopped mid-verse. We got so good at "dancing" in this way, that we just lay down when we knew the song was about to end. And we lay there with Toni until the next stanza began.

Dreaming, I sat down in my airplane seat with a weary sigh. It had been a long battle. I looked over at the empty seat beside me and wondered how I would get to Key West without losing myself inside of the grief. I woke up. It was October, four full months before our scheduled trip, only two months into Toni's cancer treatment. I knew then that when I finally went to Key West I would be alone. I shared this vision with no one in my family. I became an actress when we talked about "our trip." I pushed the memory of this premonition, or dream, whatever you prefer to call it, into the farthest recess of my mind. Without hope, there is nothing. Without faith, there is nothing. And if it had been shared, it would have shortened her life on some level. Of that I am sure.

Chapter Five

The Beauty of Grief

By January, our trip was indefinitely postponed. Helplessness blanketed us as we faced a new turn in the roller coaster ride.

Toni began to withdraw to a place where I have never been and I didn't know how to reach her. After years of experience doing just the right thing or finding the perfect gift, I found myself completely lost.

I searched for something I could do, something that would make a difference. Anything, to bring back that smile to her lips. Humor was harder to find. Still, my mind worked overtime. What can I do? What can I do? The powerlessness was new to me.

An idea came to me when she said, "you remind me of Oprah." As we talked, it became clear how much Toni admired her. I didn't know that. So, without telling her, I sent Oprah Winfrey a letter . . .

Pinky Swear

"HOT LETTER"
Ms. Oprah Winfrey
P.O. Box 909715
Chicago, Illinois 60690

Dear Ms. Winfrey:

Our family has had its share of losses. My dad died four years ago. He was one of the most beautiful people who ever graced this earth. He wasn't wealthy or well-known, but he touched peoples' souls with his humor and compassion. His death set the stone rolling.

Fourteen days after his death, I learned of my first pregnancy. I was elated. I had wanted a child for so long and somehow it made sense to me—a possible explanation for the loss of his life. Three months later, labor was induced because my unborn child had no heartbeat. The losses just kept mounting.

My sister Toni's husband, Jeff, lost his mom to breast cancer two years ago. I can hardly look in his eyes because I see my own fear reflected there.

In the early morning hours of August 16 of last year, my grandmother died. I was the last family member to see her alive. I had asked her not to leave yet because my sister, Toni, was in the hospital with pneumonia and was so afraid she would not get to see Grandma again. They had had a very special relationship. We cried because Grandma said she couldn't wait any longer. The night she died, Toni had dreamed that Grandma was sharing her hospital bed and IV. She had had her arm around Toni's shoulder and was laughing with delight. Grandma had found a way to say her own goodbye. The next day, Toni found out Grandma had died. A few hours later, we were told that Toni didn't have pneumonia, she had cancer.

Toni is 29 years old. She struggled with infertility for seven years and finally overcame it. Now, she fights the rising fear of leaving her 1-year-old daughter, Jamie. The only hope for Toni's survival is a successful bone marrow transplant. Toni and I held each other and sobbed after she (needlessly) made me promise to be a surrogate mother should she die. I know beyond a doubt that it is possible for a heart to shatter into a million little pieces and still keep beating.

After I learned Toni had cancer, I went to lean on the man that had promised to be with me in good times and bad, but he was nowhere in sight. My divorce was final on December 30, four months later.

I look at Mom with wonder. This woman has lost so much in such a short period of time, and she still puts one foot in front of the other and just does it. She lives. And she does it well. She does it with strength, courage, fear, sorrow, hope, humor and, most of all, she does it with love. A mothers' love.

People tell me I should write a book. Our losses, to them, seem beyond belief. But, you know what? I consider my family blessed. I know this is hard to comprehend. My Mom's best friend, Amy, looked at me like I had lost my mind when I referred to "the beauty of grief."

A glimpse of Heaven's beauty shines from the inner spirit of family, friends, and total strangers who have reached out to us to keep us from falling down. They've brought food, donated money, held raffles, and even stitched a quilt with a personalized square from each of Toni's coworkers at Wal-Mart. I thank God for these people who have shared our grief.

We are who we are because of weathering life's storms and reveling in its rainbows. Without losses, we would not know how precious life is. True joy would be a stranger. By being true to your soul, which allows you to really feel and love, you guarantee intense pain when it's lost. It certainly is a double-edged sword. But even knowing this through experience, I would never, ever do it differently.

That's what I meant by the "beauty of grief."

I am, of course, asking a favor of you. You are the only celebrity my sister has ever said she adores. I know she is not the only fan who feels this way, but you have connected with her somehow. It would mean the world to me, and to her, if you would send a personalized note or picture with a few words of

inspiration. I would ask that you do this as soon as possible, as Toni is not doing well . . . If you have any questions, please feel free to call me. Thank you for listening.
   Sincerely,

Some dreams are not meant to come true, but they still serve a purpose. This one gave me hope. Each day, I waited for the envelope to arrive. I eventually shared this with Toni. "You wrote to Oprah Winfrey?" she asked, incredulous. I think she realized, then, just how at a loss I was.

The support I received from my coworkers (Judy, Lori, Maureen, and Eileen) was invaluable. It allowed me time to make almost daily trips to Rochester, where Toni was treated on an in- and outpatient basis at Methodist Hospital. Accommodations were provided by The Gift of Life Transplant House, where many nights were spent building jigsaw puzzles with people that were living the same nightmare as us. God bless the people who have made that resource possible.

Although I was nearly absent from my business, somehow, my clients' needs were served, appointments were attended, and my written reports got done. Often, I didn't even have to coordinate them.

I suspect my friends at work discussed how to help me, besides the obvious work that needed to be done. A card of support, or flowers, "just to brighten your day," often sat atop my desk as an early morning greeting. When Toni's treatment conflicted with my parenting schedule, there was always some person who offered to care for my son in my absence. Eileen, whom I had befriended years earlier, had returned to the workplace with us. She helped me more than she could have possibly known when she said, "Dawn, this isn't always going to be your life," remembering her own dad's losing battle with cancer.

My coworkers also supported me by not jumping ship when, my soon-to-be ex-husband, threatened to dissolve our company, of which he was a 50% shareholder. They shook their heads in disgust when he screamed obscenities, which echoed down the second floor hallway. And they laughed as hard as I did when Steve wrote, "Fuck you bitch," backwards, on the transparent plastic that served as a temporary wall dividing our office space during the divorce. By virtue of our career choices, motherhood, or both, I was surrounded by caregivers, and they gave me their very best.

Toni's coworkers at Wal-Mart in St. Cloud took up a collection and presented her with a check for $475 just five days before Christmas. They also donated their regular and vacation hours to help with the mounting expenses. The Little Falls Wal-Mart store sent Christmas gifts for Toni, Jeff, and Jamie. "They don't even know me!" Toni said, in amazement.

These things helped keep us afloat, and because of

them, I continued to find ways to keep hope alive. It is instinctive. Hope fostered a desperate attempt to have Toni see a doctor in Texas, who was publicizing a new treatment and cure for cancer. Through "Fedxing" medical records and long distance phone calls, he opined that her cancer was "Too aggressive." He couldn't recommend his protocol. We were thrown from the coaster again.

All the while, life continues around you. There's an office to run, a toddler to raise, groceries to be bought, bills to be paid, and for me, a lesson in living alone following the divorce, to be learned. Not a good time to be alone, but there was no choice. There is nothing like death to knock down the door and tear the blinders from your life.

I began to date. As a distraction really. It felt wrong. I felt guilty sharing this with Toni. My life moving on, while hers was in limbo. Guilt flourishes. But you can't stop living. Anyone who is fighting for his or her life demonstrates just that.

Anyone who is fighting for another's life does, too.

One incident stands out like no other. I spoke with Toni by phone, at her hospital room in Rochester. Mom had prepared me. She said, crying, "Toni's not herself. I feel like I've already lost her."

Toni and I made small talk. It took no time for me to realize what Mom meant. Toni had retreated. I began asking open-ended questions, tiring of the yes and no responses. I heard her anger. "Mom's constantly smoking . . . Jeff's plugged into the television . . . All they do is build puzzles." I heard what she was saying.

I was cooking seafood lasagna for a date that evening. At that moment, the contrast between our lives was distinct. I realized she was alone, that no one, including me, could possibly know what it was like for her.

"Toni, please don't," I pleaded. "Please don't do this," I said fearing her misdirected anger would push us away. I went on to tell her how much we loved her and how hard this was for us.

She spewed back, "Oh, I'm so sorry it's hard for you."

I began to cry. We hung up with nothing resolved, but at least the core issue, her anger and withdrawal from our family, a pill so bitter it makes you gag, was out in the open.

The following morning, I hesitantly walked into her hospital room. Toni's eyes were puffy from the long hours of grief that had followed our exchange. Our arms opened to one another and we embraced.

"I'm so sorry," I said.

"No, I'm sorry," she replied.

In hindsight, was our raw, pain-filled confrontation worth it? Yes.

If I had a do over, would I draw out her rage again? Absolutely.

Chapter Six

The Final Five

My physical and emotional resources were depleted. "I have to get away," I heard myself saying repeatedly. So, on March 9, I flew to Arizona alone, with mixed feelings and guilt packed next to my toothbrush and swimsuit.

The warmth of the sun thawed my soul. I swam in the pool, basked in the sun, and dined on what the menu called "angry shrimp" and clam chowder served in a soup bowl made of bread. I rode on horseback into the foothills. I hiked in the Phoenix Mountain Preserve. I strolled the brick path through the Desert Botanical Gardens, taking the time to see the details of the desert flowers and cacti. I took MacDowel Road east to the Phoenix Museum and viewed the Frank Lloyd Wright exhibit. I wandered through the historical neighborhood of Coronado. I drove north to Oak Creek Canyon and stood with my mouth agape at the sheer beauty of the red rocks along the way. I had unknowingly traveled to one of the strongest energy vortexes in the world—Sedona.

And I ran every single morning, drinking the fresh air.

I learned something, something I thought I already knew, yet I really had not understood it fully until then. We need to take care of ourselves, to replenish our own resources physically, emotionally, and spiritually. The Japanese call it Satori—union of the mind, body, and spirit.

Three days away. That's all. It had to prepare me for what I knew awaited me at home. I dreamed I was already there, in my basement with the children, knowing a tornado was approaching. It was coming from a northwesterly direction and would hit in approximately 15 minutes. But, in the dream, the clock did not measure the time; it was measured by the calendar. And 15 minutes was six weeks.

The last night of my brief escape was memorable. After a Swedish massage, I ran back to my room, with thunder and lightning chasing me. I opened the French doors to the veranda, letting the window sheers billow into the darkened room. I took off my clothes and crawled underneath the covers. As I curled up in a naked ball, I cried for my sister. And I cried for me.

I woke up, boarded the plane, and returned home. As I thought about how I would describe my trip to her, I cringed. Guilt for having gotten away slowly was seeping in. A letter from Toni was waiting for me when I got there . . .

Dear Sis,

Tomorrow you leave for Phoenix and I'm so jealous! I would give anything to be somewhere warm right now . . . I'm glad you're taking some time to take care of you. I love you so much. You mean the world to me, and there isn't anything I wouldn't do for you . . . .
Love Ya!
Toni

I was as prepared as I could be for the storm that was on its way.

∾

I have struggled with this chapter almost since the day this book was born. Maybe it is because I myself hesitate to make this journey again. It is painful and people instinctively avoid pain, though doing so sometimes merely guarantees more of the same later in their lives. The rivers of grief run deep. It is necessary to relive those moments, to swim in them. By doing so, with time and able assistance, you can let them go. If not, they will fester and infect other areas of your life.

∾

"Fucking A!!!" my sister screamed. No one in the oncology unit could pretend they didn't hear; nor could they deny its meaning. Brokenhearted, Jeff told

Toni she was going to die. At 30 years old, her life was almost over and there was no way to stop it. The clock ticked like a bomb. And every single moment mattered.

"I can't leave Jamie," she wailed.

"Oh," she groaned, "that poor girl," she said, understanding how hard her death would be on Jeff's niece, Miranda.

Jeff was sobbing openly, as Toni's mind processed her mortality faster than a computer, accepting that her life was about to end. The tears coursed down my face and my heart exploded, as I listened to her tick off the things she needed before she died. I listened in total awe.

"I want to go home. I have people I want to see," she said, dictating her list as I quickly wrote the names in pencil on the back of a big brown envelope that had been left on the hospital bed tray.

One situation, a falling out with a former best friend, needed to be set aside. "I have to see her," she said. "I need to make things right."

I asked for a moment alone with Toni. Not a small request, given there were only going to be moments left. I sat next to my sister. Our legs dangled over the side of the hospital bed, like we were on the dock again, splashing our feet. There was nothing left to say. We looked at each other, communicating everything we needed to by a mental umbilical cord.

I broke the silence. "I want you to know that my next child will be named Toni."

"You don't have to do that," she said.

I shook my head, smiling and crying at the same time. "I know," I said choking.

She got so serious then. "I want you to promise me that you will learn how to let other people help you. I am so worried about you. I don't want you to go through life all alone."

Her request scared me. She had summed up my life in a few sentences. She called it as she saw it because she didn't have time to tiptoe. And I made my promise to her, just like the promises of our childhood: I pinky swore.

A flurry of activity. No time to waste. We knew her death would come in days, having watched the cancer come back after each chemo treatment, like a flame to gasoline. The local hospice was contacted, a hospital bed was delivered, and staff were waiting for us when we arrived just a few hours after she had been told her life was going to end. I contacted Steve to make arrangements for our son, Alex, until I returned. Whenever, that may be. I contacted my office and told them I was going home to be with Toni until she died. I asked for their help in running the business, knowing without a doubt that I could count on them. I had no idea how long I would be gone. I experienced an emotional tornado akin to the one in my Arizona dream.

At a time like this, your senses are heightened to a level you have never known before. Your perspective so sharp, the bull never shits. When there's no time left, you get right down to business. There are plenty of long nights waiting for you—to ask your questions, to wrestle with the answers. But now, right now, was our time to share with her.

The headboard of the adjustable hospital bed was placed against the wall, in the center of the living room. We looked out the windows on her backyard, at the bird feeder and thermometer hanging from the maple tree. The couch was pushed against the wall to the right, parallel to her bed, so you could sit holding her hands or lie down for the long night. An antique upholstered rocking chair was at one corner of the foot of the bed, a recliner sat near the other. Two lamps stood nearby, one of which would stay lit through the night because Toni feared the darkness. A TV tray was stocked on the left-hand side, near the head of the bed. It was overflowing with the essentials: amongst other things, oral and rectal anxiety and pain pills, mouth swabs, lotion, lip balm, half-empty glasses of once-cold water, and a suction device to assist her should her saliva become too thick to swallow. Oh, no! It's really happening. Your mind whirls with the reality that surrounds you, and the understanding of this truth comes in waves. Suddenly, the preparations are complete and the wait for death begins. And you realize you're not ready. You never can be.

A routine was discussed and instituted without much formality. Someone must always be in the room with her, not that that would ever become an issue. At least two people would stay up at night to be there to administer medications and to stroke her head and whisper loving words of comfort when she woke from the night terrors. After the first two days, I didn't sleep at all. Or if I did, it was in a semiconscious state.

Initially, it didn't seem so bad. We talked, laughed, visited with friends and relatives, shared stories. But when Jamie sat on the bed next to her mommy, wanting to be held, the cruelness of this disease, the unfairness of what was happening, crushed me. Toni wanted so desperately to hold her baby. Hold and comfort her child as mothers are supposed to. Only she was too weak to hold her child at all. I looked on, helpless. The reality sank deeper for us all.

I wrote a letter and posted it on the door for family, friends, and visitors, to prepare them as best I could. Knowing how hard it would be for most of them, I suggested they each share a story or a special moment with Toni, reminding them her strength and energy were limited. This seemed to work well, and everyone on the list, even some people who weren't, got there in time to say good-bye.

Surprisingly, even Steve (by now my ex-husband) called wanting to know if he could come and see Toni one last time. She wanted to see him and he sat with her in the living room, alone, as I played with Alex outside. Toni told me later that day that she had asked Steve to stop tormenting me. They said their goodbyes, and as Steve left, he hugged me with tears in his eyes, and told me to take care of myself. It was the most decent, human, thing he had done since we had separated.

After sitting with her in the morning, I would go running down the side streets of the small town in which she lived, where her neighbors, who started bringing the food and supplies almost immediately, watched from behind their curtained windows. They knew who I was. They understood why I was running. My daily route was the old railroad tracks. It was April, but I do not recall the temperature. Was it cold? Windy? Warm? I was oblivious to my surroundings.

I'd get about halfway through my route before my anxiety would kick in. I knew when I left the first few mornings that she was coherent and, according to the signs of impending death, it wouldn't happen in the 30 minutes I was gone. Regardless, I would start to feel anxious. I would pick up my pace. By the time I got her house in my sights, I would be sprinting, in a full panic, certain she had died while I ran.

Breathlessly, I would come through the garage with my emotional feelers extended. As soon as I saw someone looking relatively at ease, I could start to breathe again. As soon as I saw Toni, I relaxed.

The fear was great that I was going to miss the moment she died. We knew it would be a relatively short wait. But, as she started to slip away, the time seemed endless. I worried about my son. When would I see him again? I worried about my business. I had neglected it for so long. Yet, even knowing I'd soon return, the pressure to get back escalated. I was being pulled apart, until Jeff's oldest sister recognized my turmoil.

"You will never regret spending this time with her," she spoke from experience. She referred to, of course, the experience of spending the last days of her mother's life with her. She was right.

~

As her death approached, we watched for the signs. Outside of the fatigue and respiratory distress, initially, it showed itself in moments of delirium. Sitting wide eyed, she reminded us not to forget "the birthday cake."

"What birthday cake?" We'd ask, shoulders shrugged.

"Whose birthday is it?" Our heads shook in united confusion.

She rambled on, and we realized she was delusional. The unexpectedness softened the blow and we chuckled. She insisted that someone close the drapes. "You know Mom," she said by way of explanation. Whatever that meant. She thought it was hysterical and roared with laughter. So we did, too. It sounded so wonderful to hear her laugh again, to see her playfulness return.

I sat a few feet from the foot of her bed, staring at my now-sleeping sister, listening to the others as they recited the comic events. The tide abruptly turned, and I was overcome by such profound sadness that I started to cry. The room was silenced, as my crying quickly turned to soul-rending sobs of grief. My body rocked back and forth, as the waves of reality crashed ashore, one after another, until Amy led me from the room.

∾

As we cared for Toni, we noticed her labored breathing, the signs that the tumor was growing. When she lay down, only one side of her chest would inflate when she inhaled. She had a hard time breathing, so we would sit her up, hoping it would help. We sponge bathed her as her body temperature rose. Soon, she was unable to talk to us. She'd try to form words, but she had no energy to speak them.

I remember one incident when Jeff and I could not understand what she was trying to tell us. She waved her hands, eyes boring into ours, trying to convey her message. We just looked at her, at each other, helplessly. Like strangers in a foreign country. She fell back, defeated, sobbing with frustration. We gave her another anxiety pill, craving one ourselves. But, we needed lucidity more. She was counting on us.

We quickly learned to read the signs of pain and fear. Her brows would start to knit. Her breathing became shallow, her legs restless. She'd whimper. These were some of the physical signs. There were other indications as well. Tension filled the air. You could feel it. Things would start to go wrong. Someone would spill something, or a light bulb would pop. It was negative energy filling the room.

Jeff had asked, more than once, how often could we give her the medications. We followed the schedule to a T, keeping a drug diary on the tray. It gave us something to chart, to focus on. As she progressed, and her pain increased more and more quickly, he would ask again, doubting we were doing the right thing by medicating her so soon. But, the signs of her struggling were returning sooner. We were told by the hospice staff to give the medication more often, or as soon as we noticed she was uncomfortable. This truth took some time for him to comprehend.

A turning point came when Jeff said we'd have to wait to give her another dose. I was dumbstruck. Then I realized the reality was still hitting him, too. He wasn't immune to the mind's desire to deny the reality that she had begun to die, simply because he had lived this with her during the past nine months.

"Jeff, they said we should give it to her as soon as we notice she needs it," I said gently, ready to cry for fear that she'd have to wait a minute longer to have relief from her pain.

"But, it's only been an hour and a half since the last dose."

"I know," I replied softly, looking at him with tears ready to fall. I remember his shoulders sagged forward and he buried his head in his hands, as another wave came crashing down. It was getting closer.

When she couldn't swallow the pills, we crushed them and used a syringe to squirt the mixture down the back of her throat. Dehydration soon followed. We applied balm to her lips, which were so dry it was like rubbing balm on tag board. We used an oral swab, a small pink sponge on a sucker stick, to moisten the inside of her lips and mouth. The saliva had gotten so thick that it coated her teeth. Her eyes stayed partly open, and we realized there was no moisture there to let her lids close.

Slowly, tugging the lid from her eye, Jeff squeezed lens-wetting drops into the dry sockets. Her eyes gently slid closed. I could feel her sigh. With his lips gently pressed against the crown of her head, he apologized, "I'm so sorry, baby."

When she started to choke on the liquid medication, we administered it rectally.

In the midnight hours, we noticed the rustle of the sheets. The signs were almost imperceptible, but our senses were fine-tuned. There was no way we were going to let the pain get ahead of her. It had happened once. We were unable to calm her and the pain was palpable. We still beat ourselves for that one.

Jeff put on the rubber glove. The sound of it stretching and snapping is still fresh in my mind. I pulled the foil back, allowing Jeff to pinch the suppository between his thumb and forefinger. Rotating it so the torpedo shaped end was pointing up, his forefinger slid into the slightly indented bottom, allowing him to guide the suppository into her rectum.

I held her legs apart. Using a flashlight, so we did not have to turn on the overhead lights, Jeff inserted the medication, which we knew would quickly relax her.

"Uh, oh."
"What?"
"I think I put it in the wrong place."
"Are you sure?"
"Yeah."
"Oh, shit."
"Well, it will still work, won't it?"
"Yeah, but . . . here, let me see."

Another stretch, another snap of a glove. Sure enough, I felt the suppository, grasped it between my two fingers, removed it, and quickly placed it where it belonged.

"Thanks."

"No problem."

"It just figures I'd do that," he said, reading my mind. I nodded in agreement, laughing with insane relief, while my sister's voice rang inside my head, "What a couple of morons."

There were other people helping, but I vaguely remember them. I mostly remember Jeff and me taking care of her. I have mental images of the amber glow of the lamp illuminating the living room at night. The stillness. It was peaceful. An occasional snort was heard from Jeff as he dropped off, immediately jerking awake, his heart clearly racing. It's a pattern of sleep that develops from long periods of unrelieved stress. After a few minutes, the fierce pounding of his heart seemed to subside, and I looked at the sleeping outline of his body under the lavender knit throw.

I began to really love Jeff shortly after Toni was diagnosed. But not because he was my brother-in-law. It was because I saw him: a stubborn, hard-ass, car-lover, turned inside out because of the depth of his love for my sister.

I was a witness to his devotion as he rubbed her neck and back, working out the tension. He massaged her feet with moisturizer with strokes as deliberate as Michelangelo painting the water-colored ceiling of the Sistine Chapel. He learned to administer the Neupogen (a drug used to increase white blood cell development), so she didn't have to make as many trips to the hospital or doctor's office. I remember hearing her muffled painful cries coming from the bedroom where Jeff injected the drug into her abdomen. He walked every step of the way with her. When she woke from her night terrors, he was waiting. Talking until the sunrays lit the sky, getting her through the darkness.

∽

It was mid-morning and Rhonda, Toni's best friend, came by again. By now, Toni was no longer able to talk, so weak we had to put a pillow alongside her head to keep it from falling uncomfortably to one side or the other. Her eyes never opened again.

Rhonda sat on the couch with a heavy sigh, the emotions caught in her throat. She clutched Toni's hand between hers. "I love you, Toni," she said, crying. Toni made a couple of guttural noises. Rhonda's shoulders shook as she wept. I placed my hand on her left shoulder. I heard what Toni said. It was as clear to me as if she had opened her mouth and spoken the words.

"I love you, too."

At that moment, I thought of my own death and made myself a promise to choose meaningful relationships so that, when I lie dying and can no longer communicate, the voices I hear will be those of the people I love. I was comforted by that promise.

As Toni lay there, I remembered something I had read or had been told. You should give a person who is dying permission to let go. Sometimes people cling to life for us because *we* are not ready to let them go. Holding her hand, I murmured in her ear that I was ready and it was okay for her to go. Without any thought, I softly began to sing one of the lullabies I sang to her as a child:

> *Go to sleep my baby child,*
> *Go to sleep my little baby,*
> *When you wake you will see,*
> *All God's pretty little ponies* . . . .

One, by one, we sat and told her it was okay to let go. One heart broke after another.

~

Her skin changed as the time of death drew near. It became almost doll-like, smooth and cool. "Watch for the discoloration of her extremities, beginning with the fingers and toes," her hospice nurses told us. Mottling of the skin occurs, a marking of blotches of different shades of color, as if it were stained. As you wait, the days turning to years, you look for the signs, some indication that this won't go on forever.

My mom smoked nonstop, three cigarettes at a

time. I hardly saw her through the blue haze in the garage. Mentally, I questioned her. Why aren't you in here with Toni? The answer came months later, as Mom sat in a rocking chair in my basement . . .

Mom brought Jamie and Miranda, Toni's niece by marriage, to my house to visit. In the middle of the night the storm sirens had sounded. We ushered the kids downstairs, to the unfinished basement. Mom sat in her nightgown, rocking back and forth, cupping Jamie's tiny head to her breast. I looked at Mom, who was a million miles away, and my mind flashed back to our house on Thomas Avenue and the newborn infant in need of a bottle. In that instant, I understood. Mom couldn't sit every moment with Toni as her youngest daughter was dying. It would have killed my mother.

"GET MOM!" I yelled.

The mottling on her head appeared out of nowhere. It was happening. The time had come. OH MY GOD! It was happening quickly. The days that had turned to years quickly turned back to only minutes. Everyone gathered tightly around Toni's bed. A mirror image: Jeff and my mom, alongside the bed, each of them holding one of Toni's hands. I looked at my brother Barry, who I had seen more of in the past few days than in the preceding nine months, standing next to Mom and I wondered, "Where have you been?" Jeff later speculated that Barry's conspicuous absence may have been because he was "scared to death."

I stood at the foot of the bed, holding Toni's foot. The gaps between our family members were filled with friends. With anticipation much like excitement, we waited momentarily for her death to arrive. The past five days finally culminated in Toni's freedom. Invisibly, the conductor waved his batons, as the orchestra, playing out her life's song, reached its crescendo. At that moment, we became one in our love for her.

Her breathing had become so shallow, it was hard to tell if she had stopped. The length of time between breaths, so long, we thought she had died more than once.

A candle in memory of Jeff's mom had burned constantly for the past five days. It flickered. The radio played softly. At 5:55 p.m., on April 25, just nine months after her diagnosis, Toni Lee Lodermeier died, as Patty Loveless sang "You Don't Even Know Who I Am," in the background.

It was that simple.

We stood gathered around her in a silent memorial, not wanting the moment to ever end. Just beginning to absorb the reality that it was over. She was gone, set free from the months of suffering. Free to fly at last.

The women moved into the kitchen and the funeral

director was called. The men remained in the living room, talking. Even here, the rituals go undisturbed. Jeff removed the catheter. I stood alone with the men in the living room, back against the wall, looking at my dead sister. I noticed her toenails. They hadn't wanted her to wear polish during her treatments because they needed to be able to monitor her oxygen levels in her nail beds. I left the room.

I came back with the polish. The men exchanged surreptitious glances that said of me, "she must be in shock." So, I lied. "Toni made me promise to paint her toenails." That's all it took. With noticeable relief, they accepted my explanation and I got to paint my sister's toenails one last time.

As I finished, they asked if I were going to paint her fingernails, too? They didn't know it was only the toenail painting we had shared. So I found some clear polish, and two of Jeff's brothers stood holding her hands as I completed the job. It was a little something else we could do for her.

I stood rooted in the living room, spending every last minute with her, as they lifted her body onto the gurney. The body bag was pulled up and zipped closed. I didn't know the bags were red. I noticed the corner of her pajama top hanging out of the bag, as she was wheeled from her home. The calico print. Small pink flowers with baby blue centers on a background of white. Unnoticed by the others, I moved to the sidelight window of her front door, mesmerized by the image. The pajamas she wore had been worn by both me, when I was carrying my child, and by Toni, when she carried hers. I watched as the wheels of the cart rolled over the cracks in the driveway, fluttering the material as if she were waving to me. And I waved back.

Chapter Seven

The Wound

After Mom went to bed that night, Jeff and I sat up and talked. After what seemed like hours, we decided to call it a night. I went upstairs, only to turn around and go back down to use the bathroom. Padding barefoot through the kitchen, I headed for the bathroom, guided by the illumination of the night light there.

I could see as I walked through the kitchen that the living room was already dark. I thought Jeff might still be sitting in there. If so, I wanted to respect his privacy, so I did not glance in that direction as I came through the door from the kitchen into the hallway that led to both the bathroom and where he sat.

Unbeknownst to me, Jeff was standing in the dark hallway, turned towards where Toni had lain. "Goodnight, honey," he whispered softly, turning towards the door at the precise moment I was coming through it. We collided in the dark.

The rush of adrenaline made me scream and break into a cold sweat. Jeff's entire body sprung. His arms swung out and upwards, as his feet left the floor. It was the only time in my life I'd heard a man scream. Really scream. And for a brief moment, he resembled a 6'3" hummingbird.

We were unable to speak, gasping for air, our hearts jackhammering in our chests. Slowly, we recovered. And when we could fill our lungs with air again, laughter came rushing out. And we stood in the hallway, five feet from where Toni had died only hours earlier, and laughed. It got louder and louder until we were hysterical. Laughing until we cried, our bodies shook from the rush of adrenaline.

"You know who did that, don't you?"

"Yeah."

"Oh, no. She's at it already."

Toni had threatened to haunt us if she died. We suddenly realized how vulnerable we were, as the list of stunts we had pulled on her flashed through our minds. Mom woke, she told me the next morning, not to the synchronized screaming, but to the ring of our laughter. She smiled at the sound, turned over, and went back to sleep.

Before our run-in, Jeff and I were wound tight from the roller coaster ride that had begun nine months earlier, concluding with the intensity of the past five days—so tight, there was little to no hope for sleep. The midnight collision released the tension from our springs and afforded us the rest we so desperately needed in order to begin to learn how to live in this life without her. We both slept like babies.

Knowing that experts advise you not to make any significant changes in your life after you have gone through a traumatic experience, Jeff helped me to purchase a 1974 (T-top) Corvette the day after the funeral.

"An investment," we agreed, laughing as the wind rushed past us at 90 mph.

Looking back, I think we were both in shock, combined, of course, with the relief that the whole ordeal was over. It was an ending we hated, but it was finally done. The stress could begin to dissipate. And with the release, came a weariness that was overwhelming.

A few days later, Mom told us she had been stirred from sleep by a tapping on her shoulder. "Mom, don't worry. I'm all right," she heard Toni say. It has brought her immeasurable relief ever since.

Jeff told me how he and Toni had discussed, as they drove home from Rochester after she was given her death sentence, how she would contact him after she died. He had tugged on his right ear and said, "Make my ear itch." After her death, his right ear rang incessantly for months.

When we called Sister Margeen, at the Gift of Life Transplant House, to tell her Toni had died, we were startled to learn that Toni wasn't delusional when she told us not to forget "the birthday cake." She was still taking care of business. Toni died on Sister Margeen's birthday.

One of Toni's favorite nurses was named Ginger Rogers. We joked and thought nothing more about it until the famous Ginger Rogers died. The same day Toni did.

Of course there are many plausible explanations for these experiences, and some will write them off as merely coincidental or ironic. Just like when Jeff was at the funeral home making the arrangements and randomly selected a memorial card from a box containing at least 100 samples. He brought it towards him, quickly recognizing it as a card he had read before. It was from his mother's funeral three years earlier.

And our minds can certainly play tricks on us. About one week after Toni died, Jeff woke from a sound sleep when he heard someone say, "Me." Then, again, about five seconds later, "Me." He rolled over to his right side and listened for Jamie to make more noise, but she wasn't making any sound at all. Then he noticed the smell of perfume. He rolled over onto his left side, but the smell wasn't there. It was only on the right side of the bed. "It was Toni," he said, knowing without a doubt it wasn't his mind at play.

Impossible to rationally explain away were the outfits that were laid out for Jamie, the dresser drawers hanging open. Or the extra blankets appearing in her crib when no other living person had been present.

~

I was disoriented in the days that followed. I would wake up baffled, not knowing where I was, whether I was at Toni's or my house. My eyes wide open, I searched for the answer. I'd hear a cough and not know if it was Toni or Alex. I was shrouded in fog.

I continued to run. It helped rest my mind and burn off stress and tension. It did more than that, though. My friends at work kept their distance when I opted to skip lunch to go running, alone. I avoided their anxious and worried looks. Judy was the only one comfortable enough to approach me, and she insisted I start eating because I was getting too thin. However, my metabolism was operating in high gear and I couldn't keep from losing weight. I remember shopping for a new business suit. Finding one that finally fit, I brought it to the checkout counter. The clerk checked the tags for pricing, noting it was a size two, down from my normal size of eight. With whining envy, she uttered, "How do you do it?"

The green-eyed admiration temporarily boosted my ego enticing me to flex my rusty charm. I brazenly quipped, "Well, first your sister gets cancer, then you file for divorce, your husband threatens to kill you, and your sister dies nine months later." The stunned look of shock on that unsuspecting woman's face erased my smile, as the horror of my story, reflected in her features, reminded me that it wasn't just a bad dream, it had been a living nightmare.

The day-to-day responsibilities slowly pull you back to reality. And, on one hand, it feels good to be balancing the checkbook and shopping for spring clothes again. But, on the other hand, it's a reminder that life is going on, and it is going on without her. How can that be? And how can I go on as if nothing has happened? The guilt doesn't die. A part of you doesn't want life around you to continue. The pain and suffering have been your companions for so long, you're afraid to be without them. It also kept her here with me. It connected us. It is human nature to remember the last thing we saw of that loved one, and I didn't want the pajama material to stop fluttering.

When you cut your finger, at first there's a brief moment of realization, but no pain. Shock, maybe. The pain quickly follows, though, burning with intensity. You cleanse it to keep out the infection. Covering it with a bandage, you treat it with care to allow the wound to heal. Sometimes, red with infection, it will drain. But at some point, you remove the covering to let the wound breathe. You're hypersensitive to hot water or touch, and very cautious, frightened of cutting yourself again, but slowly, the once-open wound closes. The healing has begun. With time, there is only a thin white reminder of a scar to remember it by. And days, then weeks, pass without a thought. Until the knife almost slips again.

Death cuts like a knife into your soul. And you need to take care of that wound, the loss, just as you would a physical injury—because it can be more serious. It goes past our physical beings, right into our cores, our emotional and spiritual selves. A part of you has died, too. The hole in your heart is an emotional wound. Grief is what heals it.

Avoiding grief allows infection to set in.

I returned to my life angry, so filled with pain, I'd wrap myself into a tight little ball to survive it. The people around me worried. I resented their concern. One of my most caring associates was Lori. Judy and I often teased her and suggested she give her clients pacifiers because they became so dependent on her. Though, as much as we teased her about her empathic nature, we wouldn't want her to be any other way. We frequently reminisced about one of our favorite stories . . .

> *One day, Lori swirled into the office in her usual state of motion. Judy stopped her. "Lori, there's been a crisis on one of your files," Judy said, explaining that one of Lori's clients, a hothead with a history of assault and incarceration, had taken his coworkers hostage and was holding them at gunpoint. He wouldn't negotiate with the SWAT team and was asking for Lori.*
>
> *Lori stood rooted to the spot with her mouth*

hanging open, unable to believe what had happened. I reassured her that the client's psychologist did not think he would harm Lori and the SWAT team had a bulletproof vest for her to wear. All of this, we told her, had taken place while she was out on a medical appointment with another client. "We tried to reach you at the doctor's office, but you had already left," we said.

I handed Lori the case activity notes, where we had recorded all the developments of the day. She was unable to form any coherent thought or sentence, completely knocked off balance by this unusual turn of events. "Lori, they are waiting for you," I prompted her, while she was thinking to herself, "Why isn't Dawn going with me?" The answer was clear minutes later when she got in the car to leave, as Judy, Maureen and I looked on from a window in our office building. On the car's dashboard was a sign—"April Fools!"

It seemed perfectly fair for me to show my affection for Lori with my practical jokes. But, it bordered on criminal for her and her cohorts to turn their affection toward me as I hardened from my grief.

Sandy, Lori's mother, affectionately known as "Scooby," had stopped in at work to say hello. Before Scooby left that day, she gave me a big hug and told me to take care of myself. "Lori's worried because you are not talking to anyone," she added. My forced smile stayed plastered on my face, as I said good-bye, already feeling the anger beginning to boil and spit, like lava inside me.

Mentally, I thought, how dare she! How am I suppose to talk to her, or anyone, for that matter. Lori only got the highlights of the past nine months. She doesn't know how hard it was. She has no idea what kind of pain I'm in. Who does she think she is, judging my response to the death of my sister! Damn her for making me question myself. I know I am not doing well. How could I be? My God, my sister is dead!!! Where does that leave me? "Who am I?" I wondered, having lost a significant part of my identity.

It's the people who care that ultimately pull you through some of this extraordinary pain. Their love helps to heal your loss.

I drove home from work that day to an empty house. Alex was with his dad. I pulled into the garage and closed the door using the automatic remote control clipped to the visor, and for a fraction of a second, I hesitated before shutting off the engine. Lori's concern cracked open my infected wound, and as it drained, I unleashed my fury.

I sat in my truck, inside my closed garage, with the engine off. A double layer of insulation. A safe place for me to let down my guard where no one could see. I wasn't ready to share this. I was still doing it alone.

At first I screamed in anger, my face contorted. Oh, it felt so good to release my wrath. Then with clenched teeth and fists wrapped tightly in balls, I physically erupted and began pounding the steering wheel and dash. "I hate you. I HATE YOU!" I shouted repeatedly at God. I lost awareness, consumed by a rage I have never before understood.

Slowly, I heard myself, the sound of my voice shocking. It frightened me. My anger dissolved, and was replaced with raw pain so severe I wanted to die. The hole in my heart burned that badly. A wall of grief came crashing down so hard, I clutched the steering wheel for support, and lay my head against it, wailing, as my emotional wound bled. The wracking sobs subsided. Moaning from the emotional pain, I cried, sadly crooning, convinced that God had forsaken me. Hours later, I forced my exhausted body from behind the wheel, went into the dark house, and collapsed into bed, completely empty.

You can mentally, even physically, prepare for death, but your wounded soul will still need time to heal. That's the pat answer given by the people around you, a common inscription in the cards of condolence. The words make you flinch because the time it takes is painful. It hurts. There is no plan or schedule to follow. You find yourself on your own. It's the transition from life, as you once knew it, into the unknown.

I thought I was prepared for Toni's death. But the aftershock, fog, anger, and intense pain were all necessary. It made it real. Weeks later, I saw my first glimmer of hope returning. A sign of life.

On Mother's Day, I ran in the "Race for the Cure" of breast cancer. I fantasized about winning it for Toni but almost killed myself trying. I was running hard, as fast as I could, from the loss of my sister—a race I should never have run—as surely as I ran toward the finish line.

Later that day, I sat with my son, at the time 2½, by a pond near our home. He unpacked our snacks from beneath the seat of his plastic trike and, sitting side by side, we ate fruit snacks and drank from juice boxes. My thoughts turned to Toni this Mother's Day.

Mentally picking up on this, Alex looked to the pale blue sky and said, "Hi, Toni." I was caught off guard. Totally unprepared. My breath was caught in the sudden constriction of my throat. "Hold on," I warned myself. Hearing no response, he looked my way with a furrowed brow.

"Say hi to Toni, Mom," he said, admonishing me. Holding on as tightly as I could, I choked out a greeting to my sister. With a smile of satisfaction, he took another bite of his fruit roll-up. The strangle hold around my throat slackened. The moment was passing. Looking heavenward, he added, "We miss you, Toni," and the dam broke.

Birds flew overhead. The sun's warmth rose from the ground, carrying with it the fragrance of dry leaves. The smell of dirt was strong. I looked down at the sky as its mirrored reflection in the pond shimmered like a sapphire jewel. And as I grieved, I took in all of this, my senses alive. I looked over at my son, my beautiful son; I was filled with a spasm of love so pure I ached with pleasure. He sat unconcerned with my tears. I realized, once again, how closely joy and sorrow are related, as they danced around me.

We stood to leave our impromptu picnic. I bent down, grasping the corner of my oversized jean jacket we had used as a blanket. Fresh coffee-colored stains had seeped through. Perplexed, I turned over the jacket. Recognition followed and I started to laugh. Alex joined me, having no clue what I found so funny, but loving the melody of my laughter again. I saw myself earlier, grieving, while unknowingly sitting on top of fresh goose shit.

And the wound began to heal.

I returned to life a little stronger. While happiness was still a forgotten state, I had begun to smile. Though it didn't reach my eyes for many months, nevertheless, it was another sign of life returning.

∽

I remembered a trip I had taken, two years before my sister's death, with Grandma, Mom, and Toni . . .

> *We had gone to the Red River Valley where Mom was born and raised. As we traversed across the flatlands of Northern Minnesota, Grandma recited*

her memories of marrying her husband and raising her children.

Toni asked her if it were love at first sight when she met our grandfather. Grandma was sitting in the front passenger seat. With the video camera lens trained on the side mirror, I captured her response: "I wouldn't go that far." Our laughter was caught on tape. Mom showed us where she rode her bike, where she held her first waitress job, and the coliseum where she danced with the boys. Oh, the things we learned.

"Stop!" I exclaimed, pointing to the field of zinnia flowers to the right. A small farmhouse stood off to the left. Stirring up dust, Toni pulled the car onto the shoulder of the dirt road, and I jumped out with my camera. In the midst of the farmland stood an enormous field of breathtaking, multicolored zinnias, which, we discovered later, an 80-year-old woman had planted by hand. I snapped one picture after another, the utter beauty of it never fully reaching the photo. Instead, it was indelibly etched in my mind.

I was reminded of that beauty, our trip, as the zinnias I had planted in memory of Toni blossomed in the garden outside my kitchen sink window. I stared at the jamboree of flowers, letting them soothe me. And my smile grew along with them.

Pinky Swear

∼

It's the little things you do that make the pain more bearable. Keeping the memories alive is important. The memories are all you have and they nourish your cravings to see your loved one again. They're food for the soul, salve for the wound.

As the days turn to weeks, you find your life looking much the same as it was when you were first pulled from it. Like a split seam, the details are visible and need mending.

Three weeks after Toni died, our office lease in Roseville expired, so Chicilo & Associates, Inc. found a new space. We looked forward to the move, especially considering that my ex-husband and I still had office space in the same building. Yuck. A fresh start was definitely in order.

Still exhausted, but able to focus on the tasks at hand, I sat at my desk. A build-out of the space was necessary, so my office was still under construction. I had no door. The walls around me were sheet-rocked and taped, ready for primer. My office supplies were in boxes surrounding my desk.

Maureen, my associate, asked to speak with me as I passed her office. "Please, close the door," she said, nervously hesitant. I did so, knowing I wasn't going to want to hear what she had to say.

Maureen had joined our group a few years earlier. She did excellent work assisting our disabled clients in returning to competitive employment. Maureen loved a good laugh but never at the expense of someone else. She was frugal and health conscious. We teased her about how she packed her client files in paper bags and carried them inside those two-handled plastic grocery bags, calling her the bag lady. Our nickname for her was "Moline."

Moline performed altruistic acts of kindness. I remember one particular client who was in dire straights financially. This client had found an envelope, filled with cash, in her mailbox and she asked me about it. I did not know who had left it for her until I mentioned it to Moline, and the look on her face said it all. That, in a nutshell, was Maureen.

So it was with these memories and thoughts of her that I closed the office door, as she requested, and sat across from her at her desk. "This is hard for me to tell you. I know the timing is terrible. But, I have found another job," she said, sincerely regretting what she had to do. The stress of Toni's disease, my divorce, and my ensuing grief, were all too much for Maureen's gentle soul to bear.

The people I work with are a second family to me. Our bonds are strong and we share to our cores each other's victories and defeats, our happiness and sorrows. As she spoke, I stood up. Strangled by yet another loss, I shook my head, unable to speak. I opened her office door and fled down the hall, crying. A very professional response, I know, but she was like . . . a sister to me.

I have always wondered what "rock bottom" was like. You hear people reference it. I never thought I would experience it.

I sat in my office, with no privacy, no insulation from others' eyes and ears, letting the tears fall as I stared out the window. I was totally defeated, had no energy left. At first, I struggled trying to get my focus back. But I just stared at the papers in front of me. Then I quit trying. I gave up. My office resembled my life and the irony stung. "How appropriate," I thought to myself.

Judy tried to console me, but I was too far down to reach. Looking back on this, I'm sure she felt very much like I did when Toni had withdrawn. The minutes turned to hours, and I continued to weep. The pain and sorrow pouring from my soul, unabridged, as the wound, again opened, bled out once and for all.

Lori returned from an appointment outside the office. Unaware of the developments that had transpired in her absence, she innocently walked back to my office to say hello. Seeing my agony, her facial expression instantaneously changed to alarmed fear.

"What?!?" she cried out.

"Maureen gave her notice," I replied flatly, the tears never stopping with this interruption.

The Wound

Lori came around to the side of my desk. I stood up and she embraced me.

"It will be okay," she said. I was sobbing, nodding my head in agreement, but not feeling that way at all.

"I feel like I am losing everyone I love," I said, choking, gasping for air between sobs.

"Well you're not going to lose me," she said. And at that moment, it was precisely what I needed to hear. The losses had come too close together, and I realized I could no longer face them all alone.

After that, the only way to go was up.

I walked to the mailbox without anticipation of a letter or card from Toni. Those days were gone. The only question would be how many pieces would go directly in the trash. Hopefully, all of it. The novelty of paying bills again had worn off.

A card! All right. I felt more than a fleeting spark of excitement. Well, at least it's a card from, someone. I avoided looking at the return address, savoring the anticipation. Much too much time had passed for it to be a straggler's sympathy card. Tossing the junk, I sorted through the bills. Finally, I turned to the card.

Sliding my finger under the edge of the flap, I gently tore it open. I tugged it from its sheath. Turning it over, I let my eyes scan the words. It was naughty and I snickered, loving it. With apprehension, I read the personalized note. My heart fluttered. The card was from David, a man whom I had begun to date with some regularity. We had met through a mutual business associate. I found myself caring for him more than I wanted, or was ready, to. Toni flashed through my mind. And remembering the promise I made, I took a deep breath, and read the words again.

This time, I let myself feel his message, allowed myself to feel my own response. And if you had been there, you would have seen the smile finally reach my eyes.

Moments of happiness slowly returned. I began to notice the living beauty of the world around me, as if I had never laid eyes on it before. The colors were never this bright, were they? The smells are stronger, aren't they? I tasted familiar foods as if for the first time. It is similar to returning from vacation and seeing your home, your abode, in a different light—noticing all of the forgotten details, feeling the comfort of your nest.

Touching death wakes you up to life. The buds burst, unrolling their tender, fleshy leaves. I noticed the tips of the green blades of grass poking through the soil. I noticed this without trying. The black-capped chickadees, perching on the feeder, so cute, I yearned to cup one in my hands and blow on it, to rub its soft feathers against my cheek.

As I recovered from my loss, I would periodically read again one card of sympathy that had touched me deeply:

"The Rose Beyond The Wall"

Near shady wall a rose once grew,
Budded and blossomed in God's free light,
Watered and fed by morning dew,
Shedding its sweetness day and night.
As it grew and blossomed fair and tall,
Slowly rising to loftier height,
It came to a crevice in the wall
Through which there shone a beam of light.
Onward it crept with added strength
With never a thought of fear or pride,
It followed the light through the crevice's length
And unfolded itself on the other side.

The light, the dew, the broadening view
Were found the same as they were before,
And it lost itself in the beauties new,
Breathing its fragrance more and more.
Shall claim of death cause us to grieve
And make our courage faint and fall?
Nay! Let us faith and hope receive—
The rose still grows beyond the wall,

Scattering fragrance far and wide
Just as it did in days of yore,
Just as it did on the other side,
Just as it will forevermore.

(From the writings of A.L. Frink)

This message of sympathy had also been sent by Dave. The one who, months later, would ultimately renew my passion for all things . . . my faith in words. Though I was unaware of it at the time, the seed of love had been planted and in my heart it began to grow.

Chapter Eight

Seasons of Grief

As you heal from your loss, you fear you will forget. Shortly after my dad died, I was driving on the interstate, my thoughts turning to him. But I couldn't see him in my mind. I drew a blank when I tried to recall his face, what he looked like. The sound of his laughter had also slipped away. I panicked. The more I tried, the less I remembered. Like mercury, I tried to grasp it whole, but it kept splitting apart into smaller beads. The greater my desire to clutch it, the faster it darted away. So instead of returning to the office, I drove home and pored over every picture of him I could find, examining them one by one to absorb the details. With closed eyes, I checked my mental image. Satisfied I wouldn't forget his face again, I returned to work with a picture tucked safely in my purse.

It wasn't like that after Toni died. I quickly placed photos of her around the house to avoid such an anxiety attack. My fear was more for the children. Would Jamie remember her? Probably not in the sense that we think of memories. Perhaps by feeling or hearing a particular rhythm of speech or distinctive smell, she does remember.

When I see Jamie, she races into my arms like she's been waiting years for my arrival. I am the closest person, biologically, to her mother. I am more like Toni than any other woman. And somewhere in this 1-year-old's subconscious mind, she remembers her mother. She makes that connection and often tells me, "You could be my mommy."

I wanted Alex to remember his Auntie Toni. I framed a picture of her and put it in his room. He looks at it and knows her name, knows that she is Jamie's mom. He knows she is my sister and that she died, but that's really all he remembers. That, and the word cancer. He doesn't remember, as a 2-year-old, waking up in his crib and calling out, "Someone was in my crib, Mommy."

"No, honey, it was just a dream," my answer.

Shaking his little head in disagreement, he said, "No. They were sitting right here," pointing to the exact spot alongside his crib rail.

Alex doesn't remember that, but I do. It's reassuring.

But in other areas, the fears run rampant. I was excessively worried about the business; decision-making became a laborious task, and taking risks was nearly impossible. After my private lesson in how uncertain life can be, I realized anything could happen, and it could happen to me. Like a wary rabbit, I was frozen in my tracks.

You learn to live with the fear of cancer, feeling your breasts for pea-sized lumps and your nodes for swelling. You pay close attention to physical changes. A pelvic exam found a cyst in my cervix. "It's nothing to worry about," the nurse practitioner told me. Yeah, right. And you know, you just know, that the fatigue you feel is from the cancer growing within you. And sometimes that fear drives you to the clinic, where you sit waiting for the doctor to hold your hand and tell you that you don't have cancer. And you walk out realizing this is almost as bad as the roller coaster ride you found yourself on months before. Sometimes, it's worse.

Along come the "firsts" without your loved one. Birthdays, Thanksgiving, Christmas, the list never ends; it just repeats itself. My first birthday without her brought a collector car calendar and socket wrench set from Jeff. No semblance of past birthday gifts. Just as well, really, because life was so different without her, I preferred to keep the contrast distinct. A way to keep me from forgetting: a visual reminder hanging from my kitchen wall.

Most of us have experienced this. Gatherings with family members, where the void is visible. It helps to ease the loss when there are other people around to share it, recognizing and reminiscing about the person helps to fill in the missing piece of the puzzle.

When you experience a "first," alone, the nail is driven deeper.

Strolling my way through the aisles of the grocery store, slowly pushing the cart, I enjoyed what I once considered a chore, still appreciating the simplest things in life, finding pleasure in them. I selected a can of cashews, whole cashews, as a treat to myself. I set it in the cart and sauntered along, glancing to the left side of the aisle. My eyes met the greeting card section titled "Sisters." I groaned from the impact of the reality. And for a long time afterward, I was careful to avoid that aisle, like an acquaintance with whom I didn't want to come face-to-face.

The days melted into weeks and then months. I would have flashbacks of Toni's and my childhood as I watched my son grow. Alex sat on the top bunk, dangling his stuffed animals by their tails over the side. I lay on the bottom, trying to grab them. I waited for another furry critter to tempt me, but he sat silently above, plotting. I bent my legs underneath the top mattress and without warning, extended them, bouncing him up and down. He squealed from the unexpected act and, giggling, asked me to "do it some more, Mommy," never realizing that I had lost consciousness to a childhood memory of my own.

The memories do come back, over and over. You just have to find the keys to unlock your mind. And the memories comfort you, especially when you physically long for your lost loved ones to be here with you in this world. The memories reassure you that they won't be forgotten. That you won't be forgotten. You become intimate with mortality. And this intimacy begins to shape your life—if you let it.

The seasons of grief hold their own moments and memories. The anniversary of the diagnosis passes with acknowledgment and surprise that it was just one year ago . . . The memories that follow that moment are linked to the seasons, the environment around you.

The fall of her diagnosis was filled with fear and, subconsciously, I remembered. Physiologically, my body went through its response to the external stimuli. The fall colors jogged my most recent memory of that season, and with it came free-floating feelings of fear. Then came Halloween. The costumes reminded me of hers and how sick she looked that Halloween underneath her wig. She was Dracula, which was the perfect guise because her pallor was the color of death. I felt "sick" remembering.

People have come to accept and even expect that the anniversary of a loved one's death will bring it all home again. It certainly does. But it starts well before that. If you can be consciously aware of the triggers that awaken you, from a physiological standpoint, then you will have a broader understanding of yourself and others.

As I recovered, the love in my life grew, filling the void in my heart. Dave and I approached our deepening relationship with cautious optimism, having both experienced unsuccessful marriages and past relationships. Shortly before we committed to seeing each other exclusively, we introduced our three boys to one another. Alex was 3½ when he met Dave's two boys—Chris, age 6, and Scott, age 9. And as our children began to develop feelings for the new adults in their lives, and for each other, the stakes went higher.

But letting our love grow was a challenge. My struggle was intense. I mentally constructed brick walls as protection from future pain and suffering, not knowing those walls would only guarantee more of the same. I didn't yet know love was the means by which I would become whole again. Once I was securely nestled inside my unsafe shelter, I would be drawn towards the light surrounding the door to life. Then the promise I made Toni and myself would echo off the walls, and the understanding that death is the only cost of living, would taunt me. So I would tear down the bricks one by one and venture out again, in search of love and a happiness I have never known before.

Just as I would find myself understanding the mystique of this thing called love, something would suddenly make me retreat behind my sheltering walls. I repeated this process over and over again, as I withdrew for fear of more loss, and charged out for fear of missing life.

I remember making love and reaching such heights in our ecstasy that, overwhelmed by the emotional release, I wept. I explained to Dave that I had never known this kind of love before and the depth frightened me. My greatest fear was to risk my heart again. "Take all the time you need," he told me, beginning to fear that he would lose me. The next day, I received a message from Dave. He wanted to let me know that if I needed some space, he was comfortable with that. Of course, however, the message I selectively heard was that he needed space, so I began to retreat. This advance retreat behavior was exhausting and began to tear me apart because I hadn't yet let go of my sister.

I was clinging to the Patty Loveless song that played as Toni died, almost in an effort to recreate the sadness I had felt then. It was harder and harder to cry, to arrive at the depth of feeling I had once experienced. And it scared me. I didn't want to let go. I was afraid to. If I did, then I'd be without her. What would keep her here with me? What if my memories of her faded? What if I forgot her?! I felt I owed it to her to retain some measure of misery. And this unhealthy clinging to grief tore at my own happiness. The turbulence set my head and heart spinning out of control. Bit-by-bit, love was replacing grief. There simply wasn't room for that sorrow anymore. I knew that if I didn't let it go, the grief would ultimately affect the health of Dave's and my relationship, of my own being. When I identified my soul's struggle, I understood what I had to do.

I picked up the phone and booked the flight. Then I took care of my itinerary. When I called, I could hear the question Captain Benjamin Taylor could not ask—Why? I could hear the question, but all he said was, "Sure. I'll put you down." He inquired about what kind of sailing expedition I had in mind. A lame response was all I could muster. What could I say? I quickly realized, however, that I would need to prepare him, that some explanation was necessary. The charter would simply be a waste of time if I didn't.

Dear Captain Taylor:

I just wanted to drop you a quick note to confirm that I have chartered the "Asylum" from the morning of April 26 through the evening of April 27. I will be arriving in the Keys the night before and will call you then.

I have chartered the "Asylum" sailboat once before . . . I saved the brochure because I was very impressed and knew someday I would return.

I had planned another, earlier, trip to the Keys with my sister, Toni. The tickets were purchased and we planned to sail. She was diagnosed with cancer the previous August and had had her fill of doctors and chemo. But they couldn't get her into remission and she died.

You asked me what I wanted to do or see. I told

you I am a writer and like to shoot pictures. But I thought I should let you know a little bit more about the why behind my decision to make this trip. Without droning on, I simply want to tell you that I have been searching for a way to let my sister go and turn the corner so that I can be whole again. I honestly cannot think of a better place to accomplish this than Key West.

I am looking forward to sailing and will rely on your expert suggestions in that regard. If you have any questions, please give me a call . . . .

Sincerely,

I did not know this man. I did not know this man's brother was dying of AIDS in New York. I did not know this man was struggling with issues much like my own. The circumstances of our lives created a bond between two strangers and allowed us to sail together with the ease of a lifelong friendship.

I remember telling Dave about my plans to travel to Key West alone. We sat on a bench at Circus Pizza, as the boys played in the gigantic tubes. We were discussing our parenting schedules, trying to decide when we might be able to spend another weekend alone together. He suggested the weekend of my scheduled trip. Taking a deep breath, I told him I was going to Florida. He was startled. It was only a week away.

I knew I should have told him sooner, but I couldn't bring myself to vocalize what sounded so strange even to myself. Because I'd become so adept at keeping the worst of it from him, Dave really didn't understand the depth of my grief yet and I didn't know how to share it with him.

So I stammered that I had some unresolved issues I needed to deal with. By this time, of course, Dave had had an opportunity to witness my advance and retreat behaviors, and after the first dozen of roses he gave me sent me into a tailspin, he approached the news of my trip cautiously. I haltingly added that the trip had to do with my sister and unresolved feelings. With unconditional acceptance, he said, "I trust your judgment."

The night before my departure, after hours of making love, I lay in Dave's arms and he held me tightly. He had asked for no details about my trip and my heart felt heavy. Finally, he looked deep into my eyes and asked, "Are you going to be all right?" My concern that he may be too objective or too far away to worry vanished, and my heart lifted. He did care. And he was strong enough to let me learn how to walk on my own without carrying me.

The following day, as I lay in my Key West hotel room the evening before I would set sail, I was so homesick I felt nauseous. "What am I doing?" I questioned myself. "Am I losing it?" I wondered out loud. I was alone in Key West, Florida, on the one-year anniversary of my sister's death. Alone. Precisely what I promised her I wouldn't let myself be. "What was I thinking?" I chastised myself, as I tossed and turned throughout the night.

~

Two days later, I sat on the bow of the Asylum as the sun rose, letting the Gulf air wash over my body. The sailboat journey had cleansed my soul. I had had no idea what to expect. Certainly not this. My mind replayed the sequence of events that had begun at 7 a.m. the day before . . .

The morning of April 26, I had dragged myself from the hotel bed, feeling lethargic and laughing at myself as I looked in the mirror, noting the blue hollows beneath my eyes. Not exactly a poster girl for the Hilton chain. The air was stifling, the atmosphere oppressive. "I hope you know what you're doing," I repeated. I jogged, knowing that would lift me emotionally. It almost always does. I wasn't let down.

I packed what I'd planned to bring on the sailboat in a small tote and dropped off my other bags at the hotel where I would spend my last night in Key West. The cabby brought me to the Waterfront Market, off Caroline Street, a co-op-like store with wooden floors, fresh produce, nuts, beer, and wine. A deli, fresh fish counter, and a bakery case delighted my senses. There was a fresh juice bar, with boxes of oranges, mangoes, bananas, kiwi, and other fruits, stacked alongside the wooden barstool counter—the vision of a fruit fanatic's paradise. Behind it were large framed windows, which stood open to the bay of sailboats gently rocking at their slips. The line between the water and vivid blue sky was indiscernible. The breeze blew gently into the open market. I felt as if I were part of a picture, an original watercolor, experiencing art from the inside out.

I selected raw cashews, pretzels, bottled water, and wine—just a few things to bring aboard to make it feel a little like home. The smells of the fresh pastries were overwhelming, and I selected a sampling from the case, giving in to my cravings. Satisfied with my selections, I walked the few blocks to Land's End dock, where the Asylum awaited me.

As I walked, I prepared myself mentally. Introspection is one of my strongest suits. I told myself to relax and let the experience lead me to the resolution I was seeking. "Be honest, genuine, and open," I told myself. If nothing else, it was going to be an experience. And I felt confident it would be a positive one. So far, the day had not disappointed me. The doubts from the evening before were completely forgotten. I was miles away and on the right course. Everything was back in sync. I could feel it.

As I strolled down the wooden pathway, passing the other sailboats, I sighted the Asylum.

Remembering the first time I was here, the signage, which set it apart from the other sailboat charters, which read—We Offer You Asylum. It was no wonder I saved the brochure. I realized then that there is a Master Plan, that things do happen for reasons, and that I was meant to be here, now, to do this. It gave me such relief to know that I wasn't out of my mind with grief. I was very much in mind with what was necessary, the next step.

I extended my hand, introducing myself to the man who was going to help me take that step. We smiled, making contact, my brown eyes meeting his blue. Captain Taylor, Ben, immediately acknowledged the letter, extended his condolences, and never missed a beat as he proceeded to suggest where I might want to sail, what I would see. And as he spoke, the excitement began to build.

Ben's blue eyes were electric as he described the charter plans he had made for me. His tan-leathered face spoke of a lifetime in the sun. Like a basting stitch, the outside corners of his eyes were gathered together in crow's feet. He wore a full beard, blonde peppered with gray, and a baseball cap slung low. Seeing my excitement, Ben smiled, flashing a near perfect set of teeth. With a "come with me," wave of his hand, he turned and I followed without reservation this shorts-clad gentleman to the sailboat.

We set sail on a sunny, hot day, close to noon.

Below deck, I immediately changed into a Brazil-cut, Minnesota Vikings-colored, purple string bikini. He brought me to the islands of mangrove trees growing in the middle of the Gulf of Mexico, a bird sanctuary. Had I told him of my love of birds, too? No. I shook my head in amazement. He'd brought me here not knowing I'd be a bird lover in paradise.

The conversation was as easy as the sun was warm. We anchored and I climbed down behind him into an inflatable boat. The "Gentle Ben" television shows flashed through my mind. We skipped across the water, the front of the raft slapping down with each wave. Clinging to the ropes on each side to steady myself, I was bounced up and down against the wood seat and wondered if my ass would bruise.

Soon we were buzzing through the calm water as the boat threaded its way between the islands. The mangroves grew in shallow water and their tangled web of roots exposed themselves above water level. Fish swam between and around the network of submerged roots as the sun filtered through the canopy of leaves above our heads. The water looked brown from the reflection of the trees, but it was actually crystal clear.

The deeper we traveled into the jungle-like grove, the more congested with trees it became. Soon, he stopped the motor and tied us to a grouping of the small tree trunks. For a fleeting moment, I felt vul-

nerable. He could rape and kill me and no one would ever find my body. I quickly doused that line of thought. If it was meant to be, then it was meant to be.

He jumped into the water. Surfacing, he faced me. "Do you want to swim?" he asked. Looking at the jungle around me, at the water, I asked, "Are there snakes in there?" the image of a water moccasin slithering in my mind.

He laughed, shaking his head. "No, just harmless fish."

Fish, I could handle, so I followed suit. We swam down the alleyways of water, stopping to catch our breath by holding onto the tree roots because we couldn't touch bottom.

I felt as if I were in another world, far removed from anything I had ever experienced before. It was exhilarating. I was swimming with a man I had only known for a few short hours, with little to no clothing between us. A man and a woman surrounded by miles and miles of trees and ocean water, swimming together. The sexual tension felt thick. I knew there was a time in my life when I would not have been able to withstand such temptation. And once again I found myself feeling so blessed and grateful for having found love and fulfillment in my relationship that I was able to easily sacrifice the physical temptation and detach myself to analyze the emotions that coursed through my body.

The water was cool, having gone deep into the foliage where little sunshine slips through. Noticing a chill, I turned around and swam back to the raft. I climbed in, aimed my camera and snapped pictures.

Noticing my goosebumps, he motored out of this natural tangle town and into the wider sun-drenched rivers running through the islands. He anchored in the shallow saltwater. I slipped over the side, feeling the warmth of the solar-heated water penetrating the clamminess of my skin and slowly reaching my bones. It sent the shivers through the top of my head, as I was warmed from within. I stood with feet firmly planted, toes digging into the fine sand below, while I was rocked by the gentle current.

As the last shiver left my body, I opened my eyes. I noticed he, too, had taken to the warm water and was floating downstream. I lay back, lifting my feet, and drifted effortlessly, feeling the sun bake my face and body. Letting go of the tension, releasing the stress of the past year and inhaling deeply, I breathed in the beauty of my temporary habitat, feeling the energy flow into my soul, feeding it the food it so hungrily desired.

Without words, we walked upstream in the waist-deep water. I stopped. Standing, I slowly pirouetted, visually drinking in the panoramic view. And as I completed the circle, my eyes met his. "Welcome to my world," he said.

After the swim, we sailed to Snipe Point, an island of mangrove trees that grew so large they developed shores. "The most beautiful beach in the world," he uttered. After what he had just introduced me to, I had every reason to believe what he said.

We arrived and anchored quite a distance from shore because of shallow water. We snorkeled to the beach, through chilly water, until we could stand, gingerly making our way. The bottom was rocky and uneven. Carefully, I walked toward the shore, occasionally stepping on the rounded, but still sharp, point of a budding mangrove tree sprouting from below. My feet sighed when, at last, they softly immersed themselves in the baby fine sand.

We walked along the shoreline. I looked upon the first natural beach I had ever seen, undisturbed by development. It was beautiful. In the middle of nowhere. No roads, no signs, no people. We soon came to an area where the sand had sunk, creating a pool of water, surrounded by more beaches.

"Oh," I gasped, recognizing it for what it was. He smiled, as we both lay down in nature's hot tub. "It just doesn't get much better than this," or so I thought then. I turned over and soaked up the warmth on both sides of my body. One side in

water, the other in sunshine. I felt myself relaxing so much so that I began to wonder if I would have the energy I would need to snorkel back to the Asylum, remembering the slight current that had pushed us up onto the beach.

Recognizing that I was sinking fast into fatigue, without comment, the captain stood and began to walk back towards the boat. I followed him. No words were exchanged between us. We were communicating on a different level. He stopped when we came to a cluster of mangrove trees at the edge of the beach, an inlet of sorts. Stepping into it, the water was deeper than it looked. He turned and walked into the small alcove. I was right behind him.

As I submerged my overheated body, I could almost hear the sizzle. This pool of water was completely shaded from the sun. It was as icy cold as the tub I came from was hot. And my body drank it, refreshing itself. Again, I caught myself shaking my head in absolute wonder. I was filled with pure pleasure. Once my eyes adjusted to the darkness of the shade, I began to look around me. I watched tree crabs clinging to the branches of the trees, seeming to savor the same cool haven as we. Looking at one another, Ben and I exchanged a smile. And he told me how beautiful it was to watch me soaking all of this in.

We returned to the Asylum, our hearts pumping

furiously in our efforts to swim against the tide. Pulling anchor, we sailed to Marvin Key Beach, another natural beach that changes faces with each storm that passes. It was here that my thoughts turned to Toni. Reading the signs of my new reverie, he asked whether I would mind if he tried his hand at fishing. It had been so long since he had had the opportunity to indulge, as most charters had a preplanned course and Marvin Key was not a part of it. I welcomed the time alone.

I walked in the ankle-to-hip deep waters surrounding the island, picking up shells, some of which still had occupants. I began to think of Toni again. I was beginning the process of letting go of the undue grief and saying my final farewell. But it felt forced, even manufactured. It wasn't natural. It was empty of feeling. I longed for the release, but the tears wouldn't come. Instead, I began to talk to her.

"Toni, I'm having such a difficult time letting you go. I don't know how. Please help me," I said. But there was no response and nothing changed. I felt the same. I remember thinking, "Well, don't push it. It will come in time."

It was early evening when Ben lit the small grill aboard the Asylum. A day in the water and sun creates a voracious appetite, and the smell of the charcoal burning made my mouth water. He opened two ice cold beers, which we eagerly drained. As the food cooked, two more beers were opened and we continued to share stories, events, beliefs, and insights. I talked about Toni. He talked about his brother, Jerry. We discussed marriage and divorce, children and childhoods.

Ben talked about his "beautiful" wife, Marie, and how she had changed his life, him. I began to share information about my relationship. Insightfully, he then asked me why I came alone.

I explained I had not shared much of my sister's journey with Dave, the man I love. Dave hadn't met her. The closest he came was eating seafood lasagna with me after the painful words Toni and I had exchanged by phone. He had arrived after that conversation had taken place. She died two months after we first had dinner. Our relationship did not yet exist. My grief was so intense at that time, I know it would have come between us. I was not at a place where that kind of depth could have been shared. It would have pushed us apart.

I answered Ben's question and asked some of my own. We shared other life stories, the events that created who we had become and what had brought us together at this time in our lives. It felt as comfortable as an old robe.

I moaned in ravenous ecstasy as I tore into my hamburger. The bun was toasted, the outer edge of the meat slightly crunchy. The ketchup squeezed to the corners of my mouth as I took another bite. Once again, I found myself experiencing the little things with senses heightened and enhanced.

We finished our dinner and he began to play his antique flute, first an Irish jig, then a sailor's song. Not only was he a skilled sailor, but he was also an artist by virtue of his musicianship. I clapped my hands and sang along when I knew the words. The water surrounding the sailboat was calm, like a mirror. The sun was enormous and had begun to sink into the ocean, quickly dropping from the blue cloudless sky. My appetite was satisfied and the discoveries of the day left me completely relaxed, as he began to play Bach's "Air on the G String."

His bearded profile was silhouetted by the setting sun. The moment arrived without any preconceived idea or plan on my part. It was upon me like the moment of her death. The tears immediately welled and ran down my checks as he played this most beautiful sonnet. He never glanced at me, never saw my struggle or the release. He was the background to the final scene. And looking beyond the water at the setting sun, I said, "Goodbye, Toni," letting her go as the flute music skipped across the Gulf.

The following morning, April 27, started slowly after a night of restless sleep. My expectation that sleeping on a sailboat would somehow rock me to sleep, simply because the concept was exotic, fell short. The moonlight had shone brightly through the cabin door, illuminating the closet-size sleeping quarters. I heard Ben pacing above. I doubt he slept much either. The waves breaking against the side of the boat was an unfamiliar sound, waking me like a knock on the door.

With relief, I rose as the day began to break. On deck, I waited patiently for the sunrise, glancing towards his blanket-wrapped figure, now sleeping. The sun began to light the sky and paint the clouds. They looked almost like embers in a fire, the sun outlining their edges like flames.

My mission completed, I sat on the Asylum's bow, writing down the events that had taken place since I began this journey two days ago. My emotional load was now so light, I felt buoyant. I was free enough to fly, so Ben let me. I sailed the boat alone, across the Gulf of Mexico, as he occupied himself below, letting me try my new set of watery wings.

It took us five hours of sailing to return to Key West, fishing, bird watching, and island hopping along the way. I had accomplished what I had set out to do. I was ready to return. To return to the southern-most point of the United States, and, from there, fly home and return to my life, whole again.

As we sailed through the waterway back into the marina, on impulse, I stood on port side and poured a gallon of fresh water over Ben's head, christening him the "best captain in the world." He followed my lead and poured a gallon over my head and christened me the "best chartress in the whole world." We were giggling like children and I was overcome by a feeling of love for him for taking me to the places where my soul could heal, for helping me to get past the pain and grief, for sending my sister off with an exit that deserved a standing ovation. From my heart, I thanked him for those gifts so few ever give another, let alone a perfect stranger.

Back at the hotel, as I rode the elevator up to my room, my excitement began to build. I longed to hear Dave's voice. With fingers shaking with anticipation, I dialed his number, expelling a sigh when I heard him answer. I wanted to weep, from just hearing his voice, one of the most beautiful sounds absent from this venture.

Dave's car had broken down earlier, and now he was standing in the water from the refrigerator's broken icemaker, which had run all over his kitchen floor. But he no longer cared. I was on the other end of the phone line, and he felt as elated as I did.

"I love you, sweetheart," he said.

"I love you, too," I responded, as the room around me rocked only partially from my sea legs.

That evening, I dined at a restaurant Ben had recommended. I took a cab into one of the poorest areas of Key West—Bahama Village.

The ambience was a delight. The restaurant stood behind a house converted into a kitchen and bar. Palm trees, chickens, and a brick path winding its way through the backyard dining room. An adult-sized tree swing hung off to one side. A tree house was converted into an art gallery. White lights were strung throughout its supporting branches. The smells emanating from the kitchen made my stomach growl. I felt like Alice in Wonderland after she fell through the looking-glass.

The food was so good, it defies description. The main dish was Caribbean shrimp, served with a mixture of black beans, corn, and tomatoes. Fried plantains and corn bread adorned the plate. The sauce, which covered the plump pink delicacies, was filled with hundreds of spices, never to be duplicated.

Dessert was vanilla ice cream served over warm caramelized banana bread. Fried bananas encircled this artwork, and it was signed with drizzled chocolate. This creation was deserving of the name, which the restaurant also bore—Blue Heaven. And it came as no surprise that I'd found myself in this earthly heaven. I had journeyed through hell to get there.

Chapter Nine

My Word

I sit here contemplating how to finish this book. How to write the final chapter. The music of our life floats upstairs from the family room below, reassuring me my life is on track. I am complete for the first time ever. I stop to listen to the sounds in our home and my mind drifts.

I had no idea when Toni elicited the promise—to reassure her that I wouldn't live this life alone—how much of a transformation it would mean for me. I had been living by an unspoken creed that love was an unhealthy dependency that provided no real security. I believed it was too risky to count on someone else, so I relied only on myself. The promise I made meant I would have to change my fundamental beliefs about love. I knew I would struggle and keeping my word would be difficult.

Difficult?! I didn't know that difficult was just the beginning. I had to learn new and unfamiliar behaviors and often became so frightened from the risks required, my old habits beckoned me. With as much desire as the seasick, I longed to return to solid ground. The only reason I could go on sailing the choppy waters was because I realized I would be alone, forever, if I didn't continue this uncharted journey. That was Toni's fear for me: The reason she elicited the pinky swear oath. She could see it. Now I could, too.

My predisposition to do it alone, never having learned how to trust others or ask for help, combined with my divorce and Toni's death, would have locked me into a seamless vault, had my sister not made me pinky swear. How did she know? How could she? I've come to believe that as we approach our deaths, when it is imminent and we accept it, we see things that others cannot. My sister's clarity of vision allowed her to completely understand what would have happened to me had she not intervened. So she did. And she changed the course of my life forever.

There were times when I was learning how to live this new life that I cursed her. "Damn you," I'd say hatefully, when I was so scared, I just wanted to run and hide, to feel safe again in my otherwise lonely world. But I couldn't. And she knew that. She knew I wouldn't be able to break a deathbed promise to her.

As I learned how to trust, how to let go of the fear, I had someone pushing me almost every step of the way. Judy, my best friend, was instrumental in guiding me as my life began to change direction. Before

Toni died, Judy had received a card, and in it Toni asked her to take care of me. My sister was worried about my well-being, "Because," she wrote, "I love her so much." And so Judy had an obligation to fulfill, too. And along the way, as I learned and grew, Judy would periodically raise her arms towards heaven and say, "See, Toni, I'm doing my job."

After returning from my solo trip to Key West, I wrote furiously about my experiences, beginning to piece together what would eventually become this book. I shared the details of my expedition with Dave, but not the depth of my grief or the catharsis I felt letting go of my sister. I wasn't sure he could understand it. Although the fear of this being one more potential loss still enticed me to build walls, the undue grief of losing my sister wasn't clouding the picture.

As this book began to take shape, more than one year after Toni died, I realized that there was still something standing between Dave and me, something I hadn't shared. Though we weren't living together, we had begun to alternate living out of suitcases. I was writing a book about how my sister shaped my life and the impact it had on my relationship with Dave, yet he didn't know any of the details.

So, with more anxiety than I have ever known, I let Dave read my story.

I lay in bed, sweating from the fever of emotion that burned inside me, while he sat in the living room, turning the pages. As he progressed, I began to tremble and shake, as the depths of my feelings were revealed to him in black and white. In essence, I took off my mask and said, "here I am, take a look." I wasn't sure how he would respond. If there had been an escape door through which I might have run, I may never have found out. Instead, feeling trapped and vulnerable, I agonized, fearing rejection and another loss.

I heard the last page turn. My heart went wild. I waited. There was no sound coming from the living room. It seemed like hours before he padded down the carpeted hallway to the bedroom. I could hardly breathe. Like a child pretending to sleep, I clamped my eyes shut, my body as rigid as a board.

I felt Dave crawl beneath the covers beside me. Instinctually, we moved towards one another. Without opening my eyes, I nestled into his embrace, burying my face in his hairy chest. I took a deep breath and let it out slowly. He placed his lips on my forehead. "I didn't know," he murmured, as his voice cracked with emotion—a statement like an apology for something he couldn't possibly have known. It was the first time we wept together. And I learned he was strong enough to share my grief without turning away.

I remember meeting Dave's mom and dad for the first time. It was one month after my trip to Florida, on Mother's Day. I ran in the "Race for the Cure" again; the same race I'd run alone the year before, but this time, I ran beside Donna, Dave's mom. She was 63. Dave and his dad, Roger, watched as we started out together, and waited for us as we finished. Then Roger, Donna, and I stood watching for Dave as he crossed the finish line of the men's race. Later, we had a Mother's Day brunch at JAX Café in Minneapolis and I felt as if I had known them for years. And I wasn't the only one who felt that way. I recall Donna's parting words—"You fit right in."

Introducing Dave to my family was a different matter. I was so nervous I nearly passed out as I drove to Richmond with him seated beside me, the black spots dancing before my eyes as I tried to stop myself from hyperventilating.

My anxiety was so unnecessary it was laughable. In no time at all, Mom; Jeff; Mom's best friend Amy and her husband, Junior; Rhonda and Rhonda's husband, Rick, all began to smile, giving me that look that said: "Good choice."

After our extended family left, Mom, Dave, and I, sat playing gin rummy in the kitchen at Jeff's house, where Mom still lived, helping to care for Jamie, who was then almost 3. We taught Dave how to play the game and simultaneously hit him when he laid down his first hand and with a smirk, announced, "Gin." He was no rookie.

My mom rolled her eyes and I laughed. Dave was a blast of oxygen. "Toni would have loved you," Mom said, as Dave roared with laughter for having duped us both, a veritable gin shark.

The warmth of the summer day bled into the evening, as we continued to play cards. Mom startled me when she snorted, "Good God, are you hot or what!" pointing at Dave's feet.

Unnoticed, he had pulled down his tube socks until they just covered his toes. He was rapidly opening and closing his legs, while the socks swept back and forth like a dust mop across the linoleum floor. "It's like a furnace in here," Dave exclaimed, wiping his brow.

Mom shook her head and laughed out loud, as Dave's booming laugh again filled the room. Looking right at me, Mom said, "He reminds me of your father," as the image of Dad pulling out his hanky to mop his damp brow flashed through both our minds. I grinned.

When we left, Mom hugged Dave as if she'd known him a lifetime. When she turned to hug me, she murmured in my ear, "I love him." Dave was the piece missing from our family.

∽

And it was through experiences like these that I caught glimpses of the man that lay beneath the mask—glimpses that healed my broken heart.

∽

Of course it wasn't always a fairy tale. Life is real, not a Disney movie. Dave and I have struggled with old issues and established patterns of behavior—coping mechanisms that at one time helped us survive in previously dysfunctional relationships.

I learned that I wasn't the only one with a corner on the grief market. Dave brought his wounds and scars to our life together, and for some time, was unable to share pieces of his story with me. In part, because he witnessed my earlier advance/retreat dance, but mostly because he was scared. He feared rejection and loss as much as I had. Ultimately, Dave's mask came off, revealing his true self. With this unveiling, I saw completely the man I love and learned that he was strong enough to let me do all the same things for him that he had done for me.

After more than a year of unspeakable grief, the circle was at last complete. Through the keen foresight of my sister—a promise she elicited from me, cemented with a simple childhood gesture—my destiny was altered and I had found a love as rare, wild and priceless as a ghost orchid. And in the sunshine of our love, I bloomed.

∽

I continued to write in my journal. One entry was particularly revealing about how far I had come . . .

Oh, Toni, you'd be so proud of me. I'm learning, risking, and trusting for the first time in my life. In other words, I've begun to let go and guess what? I'm not free falling. I can float!

Before long, I began to walk on my own. And with each step, I outgrew who I once was, who I used to be. Soon I found myself running, running in the right direction. And on November 30, a year and a half after my sister died, I won. I glance at the plastic trophy on our mantel, which reads:

> HOG'S BREATH 5K HOG TROT
> 1st PLACE
> FEMALE DIVISION 35-39
> KEY WEST, FLORIDA

I ran my best time because, ironically, I had stopped "running." I won because I was no longer alone. I found what I needed and Dave was right there beside me—my soul's mate.

Shortly before our marriage, Dave received a letter from Judy. And inside Judy's letter lay Toni's original card and request of Judy. With a job well done, Judy passed the baton to Dave.

My Word

∿

The melody of our life's music changes, becoming a symphony of exaggerated grunts from our family room below. I listen to the noises of our three boys, Scott, Chris, and Alex, as they wrestle with the man that completes me, the one I love. Reluctantly I let the memories sink back to be taken out again, another time. The shriek of an attack, the giggle following a tackle, mixed with the huffing puffing of the man that gives love so freely. The intensity of the notes escalates, culminating in the inevitable burst of tears when the amateur world wrestling match gets out of hand.

As I start to rise to comfort the injured, I look lovingly upon the comforter, in which, only moments before, I sat wrapped as I wrote. A perfect birthday gift from Dave—a quilt made from snippets of T-shirts from the races we have run together, stitched together around the embroidered center, which reads, "Happy Birthday, Sweetheart. I Love You."

And as I gaze at this security blanket of love, the symbolism of what it reflects, I have my answer. The last chapter is complete. Rest in peace, Toni, I kept my word.

Dear Reader,

I thank you from the bottom of my heart for taking your time to read *Pinky Swear: The Gift of a Lifetime*.

As you know, this book began as writings in my journal and soon took on a life of its own. While recognizing that telling the story itself was a catharsis for me, I also realized I was writing this book as a tribute to my sister for changing the course of my life.

While Toni was fighting to survive, she also began to focus on another goal—to help others. And she did.

My dream is that this book will help you, or someone you love or care about. If so, then I fulfilled one of my sister's life wishes—her parting gift to me was always meant to be shared. Although it was I who wrapped it, the gift came from her. Now, I pass it on to you.

Sincerely,

Dawn DiChicilo

Discussion-Journal Guide

Chapter One—*Toni*

1. Generally describe how you felt after reading this chapter. In particular, how did the last paragraph affect you?

2. What memories surfaced as you read this chapter?

3. The author describes the dynamics of her family to help us understand some of their individual responses to Toni's diagnosis and death. Think about and discuss the dynamics of your family as they face stressful circumstances.

Chapter Two—*Sisters*

1. Do you think the author's relationship with her sister is typical of most sibling relationships? Explain.

2. What are the advantages/disadvantages of having close relationships, and what impact do such relationships have on the survivor when the loved one dies?

3. What person in your own life did this chapter make you think of? Why?

Pinky Swear

Chapter Three– *"Can-ker"*
1. Generally describe your thoughts/feelings after reading this chapter.

2. The author describes her physical/emotional/telepathic-like connection with her sister. Have you a similar connection with anyone in your life? Explain.

3. In this chapter, the author describes "a moment of complete clarity." Give an example of this in your own life.

Chapter Four– *Key West*
1. The author recites the precise moment she decided to end her marriage amidst her sister's fight for life. Have you ever faced a similar difficult decision? What did you do/would you have done?

2. This chapter depicts the roller coaster ride of cancer. How was the depiction similar or dissimilar to your own experiences?

3. The importance of laughter and tears is described in detail. Discuss a time when you used humor to cope with sadness, pain, or fear. Conversely, describe your best cry.

4. How do you think Toni was able to help others when she was battling for her own life? Could you have done the same thing? Explain.

5. The author describes finding ways "to let the steam escape." What things do you do to accomplish this for yourself?

6. Support is critical in surviving a loss. Whom would you turn to for support? Whose list are you on to return the favor?

Chapter Five – *The Beauty of Grief*

1. What does the author mean by "the beauty of grief?" Do you agree or disagree with this viewpoint? Explain your reasoning.

2. How do you personally define hope? In what ways can we foster hope in ourselves and those we love?

3. How did you feel about the author's confrontation with Toni? In a similar situation, have you or would you have done the same? Why or why not?

Chapter Six – *The Final Five*

1. The author writes about a trip she took to Arizona to replenish her physical and emotional resources. How did you respond to her decision to take a break just then? What kinds of things have you done to restore your inner strength at a time of great stress?

2. In this chapter, Jeff tells Toni she is going to die. How would you react if you were Jeff or Toni? How would you prepare yourself to lose someone, or to die yourself?

3. The author spends a few moments alone with Toni after learning that her sister is going to die. Imagine yourself in this scene. What would you say to your sister (brother, parent, friend, etc.)?

Pinky Swear

4. Discuss what you were thinking/feeling as Toni's death approached.

Chapter Seven—*The Wound*

1. The author describes events after Toni's death that seem to defy rational explanation. What are your thoughts and beliefs about such experiences? Discuss similar experiences you or someone you know has had.

2. Discuss the guilt of survivorship.

3. If the death of a loved one wounds our soul, and grief is what heals it, why do we avoid grieving?

4. In what ways can we help ourselves, and others, to grieve?

Chapter Eight—*Seasons of Grief*

1. What things have you or your family done to keep alive the memories of those in your family who have died?

2. The author discusses "triggers" that awaken your subconscious mind to memories. Do you agree with her analysis and conclusion? Explain.

3. What were your thoughts/feelings as you read about the author's solo journey to Key West and the overnight charter on the Gulf? Have you ever or would you be able to do something like this? Why or why not?

4. What did you think/feel about the boat captain? Have you ever encountered someone who was

instrumental in an important life experience? Tell about him or her and the experience that you shared.

Chapter Nine–*My Word*

1. Do you agree that when people accept their imminent death they are able to see what others cannot? Why or why not?

2. Generally, how did you feel about this chapter? Specifically, how did the end of the story leave you feeling?

Overview

1. Describe your overall response to this book. What was your favorite part? Your least favorite? Why?

2. How did you feel about the depth of emotion and the manner in which it was shared? Explain.

3. What did the author accomplish by writing this memoir?

4. In what ways did this book change your views about death? Grief? Life?

5. Would you recommend *Pinky Swear: The Gift of a Lifetime,* to others? Why or why not?

Order Form

Fax orders: 1-800-960-7230
Telephone orders: 1-800-720-5531
(Have your credit card ready)
Website orders: *www.treehouseink.com*
Postal: TreeHouse Ink
    855 Village Center Drive, Suite 177
    North Oaks, MN 55127-3016

Name: _____

Address: _____

City: _____ State: _____ Zip: _____

Telephone: _____ E-Mail: _____

(circle choice)
Visa/MasterCard/Discover/AmericanExpress

Card #: _____ Exp. Date: _____

Please send _____ copies of
Pinky Swear: The Gift of a Lifetime.

I am enclosing $_____
                              ($16.95/copy)

Postage & shipping* $_____

Sales tax (where applicable) $_____

Total amount enclosed $_____

(Made payable to TreeHouse Ink)

* Add $3.00 for the first book and $1.00 for each additional book.

Prices subject to change without notice
Valid in U.S. only
All orders subject to availability